Public Libraries and Their Communities

An Introduction

Kay Ann Cassell

ROWMAN & LITTLEFIELD
Lanham • Boulder • New York • London

Published by Rowman & Littlefield
An imprint of The Rowman & Littlefield Publishing Group, Inc.
4501 Forbes Boulevard, Suite 200, Lanham, Maryland 20706
www.rowman.com

6 Tinworth Street, London, SE11 5AL, United Kingdom

British Library Cataloguing in Publication Information Available

Library of Congress Cataloging-in-Publication Data

Names: Cassell, Kay Ann, author.
Title: Public libraries and their communities : an introduction / Kay Ann
   Cassell.
Description: Lanham : Rowman & Littlefield, [2021] | Includes
   bibliographical references and index. | Summary: "This is the first
   public library text to look at the administration of the public library
   as essentially different from that of other library types. It also
   emphasizes the crucial nature of advocacy, promotion, and marketing and
   demonstrates how each public library can identify and meet the needs of
   its own particular community"—Provided by publisher.
Identifiers: LCCN 2020054168 (print) | LCCN 2020054169 (ebook) | ISBN
   9781538112687 (cloth) | ISBN 9781538112700 (paperback) | ISBN
   9781538112694 (epub)
Subjects: LCSH: Public libraries—United States—Administration. |
   Libraries and community—United States.
Classification: LCC Z678 .C355 2021 (print) | LCC Z678 (ebook) | DDC
   025.1/974—dc23
LC record available at https://lccn.loc.gov/2020054168
LC ebook record available at https://lccn.loc.gov/2020054169

Public Libraries
and Their Communities

CONTENTS

PREFACE

When many thought that public libraries would die because so much was online, the public libraries surprised everyone. They came back even stronger by adding new formats and developing new services, programs, and outreach to their communities. Public libraries are like no other kind of library. They serve a specific community of users, and they work to satisfy those users. This book aims to provide information on all aspects of public librarianship from their legal foundation to their organization, staffing, finances, collection development, and services. The audience for this book includes library school students, staff working in public libraries, and anyone interested in public libraries.

As I wrote and researched this book, I tried to think about what I have learned working in public libraries both large and small and both as a staff member and as a library director. I also interviewed a number of public librarians from public libraries of varying sizes to find out their thoughts on where public libraries are going. All were thinking ahead and trying to meet new user needs and requests, and some of these ideas have been incorporated into this book. I have started teaching a public libraries course at the Rutgers University Department of Library and Information Science. Many of the students are already working in public libraries, and I have been inspired by their enthusiasm for public librarianship.

This book is divided into twelve chapters.

Chapter 1 is an introduction to public libraries and a history of the development of public libraries in the United States. It is so important to understand the history and development of public libraries in order to understand how they function today.

Chapter 2 concerns strategic planning. Public libraries need to have a strategic plan so their users and their community understand where the library is going as it moves forward. Developing the strategic plan can be an opportunity to expand the reach of the public library by involving people from the community. Many public libraries have their strategic plan on their websites.

Chapter 3 concerns how public libraries are legally established, their policies, and their boards of trustees. Often people do not understand this important information about public libraries. However, it is important to know why they operate as they do and legally what rules they must follow.

Chapter 4 discusses the personnel side of public libraries—how public libraries are organized and how they are staffed. This has changed through the years as libraries have developed and need staff with an ever-widening variety of skills.

Chapter 5 concerns advocacy and related but external groups that support the work of the public library. These groups include library Friends groups and library foundations, library associations, and state and local government. Advocacy is now an important part of the work of public libraries.

Chapter 6 deals with the fiscal side of public libraries—where they get their funding and how budgets are developed. As the funding for local government changes, so changes the funding of public libraries.

Chapter 7 is devoted to community and civic engagement and outreach. This is an area of much discussion in recent years. Many libraries have been doing engagement and outreach for a long time, but for others it is a fairly new concept. Listening to the library's community is crucial to providing appropriate materials and services.

Chapter 8 is devoted to all aspects of services to children and young adults and was written by Lisa Houde, assistant director, Rye Public Library (New Hampshire). This is an important part of public library service.

Chapter 9 is about services to individual adults and groups of adults, including seniors, the homeless, immigrants, ethnic groups, and veterans. Services to adults sometimes need to be developed to serve a particular community group.

Chapter 10 discusses collections and collection development. This is an ever-important topic since for many users the public library is all about collections. The formats available in libraries have expanded throughout time and now include books and e-books, audio materials, video materials, magazines, and more.

Chapter 11 provides information on marketing and promotion. We live in a competitive world so libraries need to make themselves visible on a regular basis.

Chapter 12 is the conclusion. I am writing this book during the COVID-19 pandemic, which has changed public libraries temporarily and probably in some ways permanently. It is interesting to see how libraries have risen to the challenge to provide materials and programs to their users if not in person but virtually.

Public libraries continue to amaze me as they constantly reinvent themselves to respond to the world around them. They are both alike and different. Responding to community needs and interests is an important part of the work of library staff and administration. This is an ever-important challenge. As I already noted, COVID-19 has been a major challenge for public libraries, and its effects will be felt for a while longer. But libraries have done what they always do: they have adjusted and continue to serve their users.

Thank you to all the people who helped me gather information for this book. I especially want to thank Siobhan Reardon, Nick Buron, Richard Reyes-Gavilan, Christopher Platt, Uma Hiremath, and Jane Fisher.

INTRODUCTION AND THE HISTORY OF U.S. PUBLIC LIBRARIES

- Early public libraries
- Public libraries in the middle of the nineteenth century
- The role of women's organizations in developing public libraries
- Development of public library services
- Public libraries from the Chicago World's Fair to the end of World War I
- The Great Depression and World War II
- Post–World War II to 1964
- 1965 to 1980
- 1981 to 2000
- 2001 to today

"In the United States, public libraries serve their communities by providing free educational resources and meeting spaces, a variety of physical and digital materials, equipment, internet access, and access to informational professionals who provide programs [for all ages] and answer questions for their patrons" (Institute of Museum and Library Services [IMLS] 2020, vii). By offering access to collections, technology and community spaces, public libraries enhance civic life and provide valuable access points to various information resources that some may not normally be able to access" (IMLS

2020). Public libraries are today an integral part of American life. The characteristics of a public library are that it is maintained by a local government, supported by tax dollars, and open and free to all. There are, of course, many models for public libraries. They can be a municipal library, a school district library, a county library, or an independent library. Some are small—one room—or large with many rooms and many floors. Some are mobile units—a bookmobile or a boat. Most communities in the United States have a public library. There are approximately 9,045 active public libraries in the United States with 16,735 central and branch libraries and 619 bookmobiles (IMLS 2020). The IMLS report also states that in 2017, there was an average of 4.2 visits per capita, and for every 1,000 people in a library's service area, 378.7 attended a program (IMLS 2020). Public libraries are emphasizing their work with people and their outreach into the communities and expanding their programs and services to meet the needs of their communities. Circulation averaged 7.3 per capita with increased use of e-books and audio. Public library collections have continued to grow. The Pew Research Center survey states that

> public attitudes are largely positive about the library's role in communities. Many Americans are interested in libraries offering a range of services—including those that help people improve their digital skills and learn how to determine what information is trustworthy. People think that libraries are a major contributor to their communities in providing a safe place to spend time, creating educational opportunities for people of all ages, and sparking creativity among young people. (Horrigan 2016)

As indicated by the Pew survey, most people in a community support public libraries even if they are not frequent users of the public library. Public libraries are used by the public for information, education, and recreation. As can be seen from the history of public libraries, the development of public libraries was a grassroots effort. Communities wanted a library free and open to all. Libraries that charged a fee were not considered acceptable in this new country with its democratic principles.

Early Public Libraries

As soon as people began to settle in the United States they wanted books. Wealthy people ordered books from England and set up their own private libraries. "Less than a decade after the Pilgrims landed at Plymouth Rock, John Endicott's pioneer settlement at Salem received a collection of books that evidently were intended for community use" (Shera 1949, 245). By the middle of the eighteenth century, libraries were already in operation. The first libraries were parish libraries and town book collections. In 1731, Benjamin Franklin organized the Library Company of Philadelphia. It was a social library where people could contribute money to be used to purchase books and then have a membership to use the library. Social libraries often had space in the building for public lectures as well. Many more social libraries sprang up first in Connecticut and Rhode Island and then elsewhere in New England. Even before the American Revolution, New England had more than fifty social libraries (Wiegand 2015, 9). A notable one was the Redwood Library in Newport, Rhode Island, that received money for the collection from Abraham Redwood in 1747 and moved into its own building in 1750. The model for the social library had come from England.

Early libraries collected books that contained what they called "useful knowledge." Fiction was controversial, and social libraries tended not to acquire fiction. Therefore, circulating libraries that made books available for a rental fee or a membership fee grew up that provided fiction for borrowers. Circulating libraries were often connected to businesses such as bookstores, coffeehouses, or a store frequented by women since they were usually the best customers. The social libraries continued to develop in New England in the 1750s and 1760s, and more were formed after the revolution. Legislation passed in the states made it easier to charter a social library. Social libraries spread to the West as it was settled. They eventually became public libraries, free and open to the public and supported by the municipality since the social libraries were not well funded and could not provide enough books for a public wanting a wide variety of works. It was recognized that the public libraries provided not only knowledge but also a place where people could meet and talk about the books they were reading. As a result, the public library and the lyceum movement, offering lectures and courses, were often coupled together.

Other models of early libraries were mercantile libraries, proprietary libraries, and subscription libraries. Young men wanting to improve themselves established the mercantile libraries, where there were book collections as well as classes and lectures. Two of the early ones were established in Boston and New York. The proprietary libraries tended to appeal more to the wealthy and were based on the purchase of shares of stock that could be transferred to someone else by sale or by gift or bequest. The subscription libraries were more democratic and were based on the idea of people being able to use the library if they purchased an annual subscription.

Boston was the early center of bookselling at the end of the seventeenth century. By 1720, there were five printing presses in Boston and many bookstores (Shera 1949, 46). The Boston Athenaeum opened in 1807 and sold stock to those who wanted to join. It also offered members lyceum series with lectures and courses. The first library supported by local taxes was the Peterborough (New Hampshire) Town Library established in 1833. The first legislation for cities and towns to maintain free libraries by taxation was passed in New Hampshire in 1849 and in Massachusetts in 1851. In 1847, the mayor of Boston anonymously offered the city $5,000 if the city council would authorize a tax to establish and maintain a public library. This plan was approved in 1848 (Wiegand 2015, 25–26). Harvard professors George Ticknor and Edward Everett were responsible for drawing up the operating plans for the Boston Public Library. Their forward thinking set a model used by future public libraries. They recommended free admission to all, the circulation of books for home use, and the acquisition of multiple copies of a wide range of reading materials from scholarly to popular. Although there would continue to be a great deal of controversy about whether public libraries should collect and circulate fiction, Boston Public Library led the way by buying and circulating the popular literature of the day. By doing this they were accomplishing Ticknor's goal of educating the lower classes. The first Boston Public Library reading room was established in 1854, in a schoolhouse, and the new building was opened in 1858. The new Boston Public Library was administered by the "Board of Trustees who were given the power to control all expenditures of library funds, appoint all officers including the librarian, and fix their compensations" (Shera 1949, 156).

The Astor Library, a noncirculating public library, was established in 1849, in New York City, for those older than sixteen years of age. In 1895, the Astor and Lenox libraries merged with the Samuel J. Tilden Foundation to form the New York Public Library. The Chicago Public Library was established in 1875.

Jesse Shera (1949) identified a variety of forces that together helped to shape the public library. The first force was economic resources. No library was possible without economic resources, which were often a combination of private wealth and community wealth (200). The growth of industrialization meant that more people were in a position to donate to their local libraries. The second force was that scholars needed more books for their work. Even though America was a young country, people wanted to collect books from elsewhere in the world so they could also have a record of what was or had happened in other places. The third force was the need for universal public education and universal literacy. Libraries were seen as a supplement to public education. Since not everyone could attend school, many could use the public library for self-education, and it was recognized that this was a public responsibility. It was also thought that reading promoted morality. The fourth force was the lyceum movement, which was often linked to public libraries and provided another form of education through lectures, debates, and courses. And finally, the fifth force was the vocational influence, since it was thought that workers should also get an education. Mechanics' and mercantile libraries were formed to provide for the reading needs of young merchants and young technicians. In addition to book collections, these libraries often added educational components such as lectures and courses. But most important was that the public library was a grassroots movement, and it took the interest and dedication of a community to start the library. It was a democratic movement that had as its goal a library for everyone.

Public Libraries in the Middle of the Nineteenth Century

By 1867, many public libraries had been established. Five hundred public libraries had been established within twenty-five years after the 1849 New Hampshire legislation. They continued the practice that a library was more than a collection of books by providing space for lectures and exhibits. In 1876, the centennial of the establishment of the United States, 109 delegates met in Philadelphia to discuss the formation of a professional library association. During the meeting, the American Library Association (ALA) was established, a constitution was drafted, officers were elected, and a journal, the *American Library Journal,* had begun publication. Melvil Dewey, one of the leaders of the library movement, published the Dewey Decimal classification system in 1876, which divided knowledge into ten categories and then divided the categories into ten subcategories. This new system caught on quickly and became widely used. Dewey also recognized the need for public library staff to have more training, and, as director of the Columbia College Library, he set up a formal library education program in 1887. The program taught book selection, cataloging and classification, reference, and management. Because Dewey accepted women into the program, he was not allowed classroom space at Columbia and had to teach off campus. The library school was soon moved to Albany, New York, in 1889, and Dewey became the director of the New York State Library. Dewey pushed for standardization among public libraries such as bibliographic control, uniform cataloging, and lists of bibliographies recommending "best reading." He thought this standardization would help libraries accomplish what was the theme of the ALA: "The largest number at the least cost." Eighty percent of the 137 cities in the United States with a population of more than thirty thousand had a public library by the turn of the century (Martin 1998, 11). "Public libraries, however, were much more than repositories for reading material for individual users. Libraries had broader communal functions, including providing space for the emotional experience of community, enabling discussion groups and at the same time cultivating a sense of freedom, status and social privilege" (Wiegand 2015, 43).

Figure 1.1. The Ames Free Public Library in Easton, Massachusetts, was designed by Henry Hobson Richardson and opened in 1883. The library is still in use today. *Ames Free Library of Easton, Massachusetts.*

The Role of Women's Organizations in Developing Public Libraries

Women's groups were responsible for establishing many public libraries. The General Federation of Women's Clubs was founded in 1889, and the members were interested in libraries. Women's clubs contributed in a very tangible way to the spread of the public library idea and to the foundation of

Figure 1.2. The barrel-vaulted ceiling in the Ames Free Public Library was designed by Stanford White. *Ames Free Library of Easton, Massachusetts.*

numerous libraries in cities and towns throughout the country. Mrs. Charles A. Perkins wrote in 1904, that the clubs had established 474 public libraries (Watson 1994). Women's clubs also helped develop traveling libraries. By 1933, the American Library Association estimated that 75 percent of the public libraries were established by women's associations (Valentine 2005, 54). The women's clubs also raised money for libraries as well as encouraging library education and state library associations.

Development of Public Library Services

Delivery services began to appear both in rural areas and in large cities. In rural areas it was the state-level agency that developed extension services with deposit collections and mobile units. In the cities there were neighborhood branches, deposit collections in apartments, and classroom collections in schools. People liked having branches or some kind of book collection nearby.

Reference services began and took hold at the end of the nineteenth century, as did readers' advisory services, which remained a separate service until World War II. Young adult service also made its appearance in the 1920s. Libraries set up a separate young adult room, and librarians welcomed young adults to the library. They also worked with young adults in the schools and in community groups. They saw their role as making young adults lifelong readers and helping them on their way to maturity (Martin 1998, 49).

Public Libraries from the Chicago World's Fair to the End of World War I

As public libraries were multiplying at the end of the century, publishing was dramatically increasing—books, magazines, and newspapers. The number of books published increased from 2,076 in 1880 to 13,470 in 1910. The American Library Association exhibited a model library of five thousand books at the 1893 World's Fair, printed and distributed as the ALA Catalog by the Bureau of Education of the U.S. Department of the Interior. Even though people continued to question the role of fiction in the public library, well over 50 percent of the books circulated were fiction. "The general public and the elected officials . . . pictured it (the public library) as an educational agency, there to help people understand the world, to prepare them to function as citizens, and to gain information needed for their employment and their daily tasks" (Martin 1998, 17). In 1901, the H. W. Wilson Company began to publish an index to periodicals, the *Reader's Guide to Periodical Literature*, that indexed twenty periodicals. Other notable publications at the turn of the century were the *Fiction Catalog* and the *Children's Catalog*, which listed recommended titles, and *Booklist*, a review journal that was published ten times a year. In 1901, President Theodore Roosevelt in his message to Congress called the growth of public libraries "the most characteristic educational movement of the past fifty years" (quoted in Wiegand 2015, 53). Public libraries were looked at as a place for the middle and lower classes to learn and grow.

Andrew Carnegie, one of the new industrial giants, decided to use some of his recently acquired millions to construct libraries. Most of it went for the construction of public libraries. Carnegie's gifts made it possible for many communities to build libraries. Between 1889 and 1919 Carnegie gave $41 million to construct 1,679 public library buildings in 1,412 communities (Wiegand 2015, 94). Carnegie's requirements were that a site be provided for the building and that the municipality commit itself to provide at least 10 percent of the grant for annual maintenance. He also encouraged space for recreation in the library, such as an auditorium or lecture hall. Carnegie's donation cemented the relationship between the local government and the library and encouraged others to donate to public libraries.

Public library services began to develop by the end of the century. Children's services were developed early in the twentieth century. One of the leaders was Anne Carroll Moore who, after getting a degree from the Pratt Institute Library program, set up a children's room there. In 1906, she moved to the New York Public Library as superintendent of the Department of Work with Children. Many other librarians provided leadership in children's services, including Frances Sayers in Pittsburgh. By the 1920s and 1930s, children were one-third of the registrants in public libraries and juvenile literature was half of the circulation. Librarians encouraged the development of juvenile departments in publishing houses and set the criteria for what publishers should publish. They provided storytelling in children's rooms and developed a clear purpose, dedicated personnel, and a concentration of effort. And most of all, they promoted reading.

Before World War I there was an emphasis on bringing library services closer to the people so that it would be more convenient. Many thought that libraries were responsible for an increase in knowledge and culture among the people. Public libraries worked with immigrants to help integrate them into the United States. The American Library Association set up a

Committee on Work with the Foreign Born as early as 1918. Many public libraries removed books published in German during World War I, while others chose to keep the German books on their shelves. The war influenced the development of outreach to hospitals. "In many respects, the services public libraries offered, the physical spaces they provided and the stories they made accessible became essential equipment in many people's everyday lives" (Wiegand 2015, 105).

The Great Depression and World War II

By 1920, the United States had nearly six thousand public libraries (Wiegand 2015, 110). And "over 75 million United States residents had local, accessible services by 1920, two-thirds of the total population" (Martin 1998, 33). Between 1935 and 1941 the Works Progress Administration (WPA) gave $51 million to build new libraries, renovate or repair 1,500, and fund outreach projects in four hundred counties (Wiegand 2015, 139). With the Depression, book budgets dropped and users were asked to keep books overdue and pay fines to help the library's income and were asked to donate books. Some federal assistance helped the libraries to keep their doors open. Libraries were important to people during the Depression, and they read more nonfiction, which was called "useful knowledge."

About eight hundred public libraries opened between 1930 and 1940. The first standards for public libraries were published in 1933. A second statement was approved in 1943. A national plan for public libraries was published in 1948, and *Minimum Standards for Public Library Systems* was published in 1967. In 1980, the first of several guides to planning for public libraries was published. This planning process encouraged libraries to assess community library needs; evaluate current library services and resources; determine the role of the public library in the community; set goals, objectives, and priorities; and develop and evaluate strategies for change. Libraries were considered places where one could examine both sides of an issue.

To protect libraries the American Library Association adopted the Library Bill of Rights in 1939. This was first revised in 1948 followed by many subsequent revisions. Many libraries adopted the Library Bill of Rights. There was also growing discomfort with segregated libraries. Segregated library services in the Jim Crow South continued with a few exceptions. The first black American to speak at ALA was Thomas Fountain Blue, the director of the black branches of the Louisville (Kentucky) Public Library. In

Figure 1.3. Many public libraries designed in the middle of the twentieth century have similar architecture. *Nicole Box/Eye Em via Getty Images.*

1935, a federal survey showed that only 94 of 509 public libraries in thirteen southern states served black Americans. In the North, blacks more often used the public libraries. Branches were often de facto black due to their location, and as a result they often developed Negro history collections such as in New York City's Harlem branches. Integration of public libraries, especially in the South, was a long time coming.

Post–World War II to 1964

The American Library Association took the leadership after World War II to move public librarianship forward. A study was funded by the Carnegie Corporation—the Public Library Inquiry—and released between 1947 and 1952. The results of this study were used to document the need for federal assistance, especially for people who lived outside of cities with no access to library service. The first federal legislation, the Library Services Act, was passed and signed by President Eisenhower in 1956 and was specifically for rural libraries. In 1964, the Library Services and Construction Act (LSCA) was passed and signed, and this act made all libraries eligible for federal funds. With federal funds the libraries added more bookmobile services and made an increased effort to benefit underserved populations. The LSCA strengthened the role of the state library agencies.

As state library agencies were developed, the structures varied; some were in the Departments of Education, while others were associated with the state library. State certification for librarians working in public libraries existed in twenty-one states by 1965. The state agencies developed statewide library systems, encouraging cooperation among public libraries and providing more access to materials through interlibrary loan. By 1969, there were 491 library systems.

Librarians worked with adult educators during the 1950s, and the ALA set up an Office of Adult Education. Some of the services provided by libraries working with adult educators were for groups such as labor and older adults, discussion groups including the Great Books discussion groups, and readers' advisory services that encouraged adults to pursue their own interests through reading.

Post–World War II libraries continued to be concerned with censorship. In 1953, the ALA and the American Book Publishers Council jointly issued the Freedom to Read statement. This happened at the same time as the congressional hearings led by Senator Joseph McCarthy.

In 1963, there were 9,517 public libraries, including 3,376 branches, which served 73 percent of the U.S. population. This was an increase of 30 percent from 1945. Also between 1945 and 1963 circulation almost doubled, and 50 percent of that circulation was juvenile materials (Wiegand 2015, 191–92). The ALA had begun to lobby on a national level. In 1963, U.S. commissioner of education Francis Keppel stated that "the public library is a basic educational resource. The widespread recognition that education is a life-long process has dramatized the importance of having good library service readily accessible to every citizen" (Martin 1998, 175).

1965 to 1980

Library systems grew in the 1970s and 1980s even though there was no increase in federal library funding in the 1970s. Almost every library belonged to a system that might be a cooperative system, a coordinated system, or a consolidated system. New technology was immensely helpful in providing access across libraries to more resources.

The first of the publications, *A Planning Process for Public Libraries*, in 1980 provided a way for public libraries to do strategic planning. This publication provided guidance in evaluating current library services and resources, determining the role of the public library in the community; setting goals, objectives, and priorities; and developing and evaluating strategies for change. This was followed by other publications, including *Planning and Role Setting for Public Libraries* and *Output Measures for Public Libraries*.

Outreach grew during this period. Libraries reached out to immigrants and other groups that needed more services. English classes were offered and materials were added in other languages. Government funds were used to develop and provide information and retrieval services.

Figure 1.4. The Wallingford Public Library (Connecticut) was built in 1982, with an expansion in 2008. *Courtesy of the Wallingford Public Library, Connecticut.*

1981 to 2000

The number of public libraries continued to grow. There were 14,653 public libraries in 1980 and 16,298 in 2000. Much had changed in public libraries by the 1980s. Many libraries had online catalogs and new online circulation systems. Although libraries began buying and circulating films by the end of the 1940s, there were now many more formats of audio and video material being purchased and circulated in libraries. CDs and DVDs were now in libraries, and soon libraries would begin streaming them. Libraries also began replacing microfilm with digitized resources such as databases.

2001 to Today

At a time when people thought that public libraries would go away because people can find so much information on the internet, they in fact have thrived. Public libraries realized that they had to provide more than just print books, and so they added e-books, streaming audiovisual materials, and many other items that users could borrow (called the *Library of Things*) from cake pans to gardening equipment and technology equipment. Programming became an important part of a public library's offerings. There were more programs for children, teens, and adults. Makerspace rooms appeared where people could create using everything from 3-D printers to sewing machines. There were many more English as a Second Language classes and opportunities to connect with others and practice speaking English. Book discussion groups in person and online were available. Users liked this variety of programs and services now offered by public libraries. Libraries formed partnerships with local organizations and businesses to expand their reach into the community. They went out into the community to listen to what the community wanted and added to their programming through these partnerships. Libraries became community centers open to all, where people could meet, learn, create, and discuss the issues of the day. Even as the pandemic hit the United States in 2020, public libraries continued to serve their users through online services and programs for all ages. Public libraries have a bright future ahead of them as they continue to serve their communities.

Discussion Questions

1. What services of public libraries have remained the same, and what has changed?

2. Do you think that public libraries are usually ahead or behind the curve of social change?

Bibliography

Horrigan, John B. 2016. "Libraries 2016." *Pew Research Center.* Accessed December 14, 2020. http://www.pewinternet.org/2016/09/09/2016/Libraries-2016.

Institute of Museum and Library Services (IMLS). 2020. *Public Libraries in the United States: Fiscal Year 2017*, vol 2. Washington, DC: Institute of Museum and Library Services.

Martin, Lowell A. 1998. *Enrichment: A History of the Public Library in the United States in the Twentieth Century.* Metuchen, NJ: Scarecrow Press.

Sager, Don. 2000. "Before the Memory Fades: Public Libraries in the Twentieth Century." *Public Libraries* 39, no. 2 (March/April): 73–77.

Shera, Jesse H. 1949. *Foundations of the Public Library: The Origins of the Public Library Movement in New England, 1629–1855.* Chicago: University of Chicago Press.

Valentine, Jolie. 2005. "Our Community, Our Library: Women, Schools and Popular Culture in the Public Library Movement." *Public Library Quarterly* 24 (4): 45–79.

Watson, Paula D. 1994. "Founding Mothers: The Contribution of Women's Organizations to Public Library Development in the United States." *Library Quarterly* 64, no. 3 (July): 233–69.

Wiegand, Wayne A. 2015. *Part of Our Lives: A People's History of the American Public Library.* New York: Oxford University Press.

STRATEGIC PLANNING AND THE PUBLIC LIBRARY

- Planning committee
- Gathering information
- Library profile
- Community profile
- Mission statement and vision statement
- Needs assessment
- Analysis of the results
- Goals and objectives
- Action plan
- The next steps

What is strategic planning? Basically it is a planning process that examines internal and external factors to arrive at goals, objectives, and actions for moving the library forward into the future. Developing a strategic plan provides the library with the opportunity to expand its knowledge both of the library and of its role in the community. It can be a powerful tool as the first step in moving the library forward as well as developing new contacts for the library. With community-centered goals and objectives, the library can expand its services and programs to meet new needs and interests.

Strategic planning is a tool that both guides and focuses the way a library approaches its work. Strategic planning is needed so the library has a road map forward and has set its priorities. It provides a way to make sure all employees and patrons understand the library's mission, goals, and objectives. Strategic planning provides realistic goals and objectives, identifies library priorities, provides a way to evaluate and measure progress, and is an important element in the development of public libraries. Having a strategic plan will help the library to move forward more efficiently and effectively, to identify changes in services and collections that may be needed, and to perhaps establish new partnerships or relationships with other groups in the community. Just as almost every business has a plan that provides a road map forward to meeting its customers' needs, the library must look ahead. The library must be prepared to meet changing patron needs and have a clear route to its future. In order to develop a strategic plan, the library must first be sure that all staff members are aware of this undertaking and understand its purpose. Strategic plans should not take so long to develop that everyone forgets why they are doing it. It should be a short, manageable document that is easy to understand and implement. If the library is part of the city or county government, its strategic plan should align with the goals of its parent organization. Although many libraries try to develop five-year plans, change happens so rapidly that strategic plans for three to five years are now thought to be more realistic.

The steps in a strategic planning process are as follows:

1. Set up a planning committee.

2. Gather information—both internal and external—and develop library and community profiles.

3. Establish the mission and vision for the library.

4. Develop a needs assessment.

5. Analyze the results.

6. Develop the goals and objectives for the library.

7. Develop an action plan to reach the goals and objectives.

8. Implement the strategic plan.

9. Evaluate the implementation of the plan.

10. Plan the next steps.

Planning Committee

A planning committee is needed to guide the development of the strategic plan. It will vary by size of library and what input is important to the library. But at a minimum the planning committee should include

- the director of the library,

- representatives of the library board of trustees,

- library staff representatives,

- representatives of local government,

- representatives from the Friends of the Library, and

- representatives of local clubs and organizations.

Other representatives to consider are library volunteers and library patrons. All these representatives serve specific purposes. The director knows the most about every aspect of the library's work. The board of trustees represents the library and has a great deal of background information about the library—its resources and financial capacity. The staff representatives see the library from the inside and know how it runs. The staff also knows the library's patrons and can provide input about them and their needs. The government and community representatives, if well chosen, can provide input as to how the community sees the library and what community needs are being met and not being met. It would be useful to have library patrons on the committee so that no one has to speak for them. If the group seems too large to work effectively, there can be a smaller steering committee that does much of the initial work.

Gathering Information

Gathering information includes both internal library information and external community information. All this is important in making decisions about the library's future. Current information plus, when available, historical data can help those working on the profiles to see how the library and its community are changing as they plan for the future.

Library Profile

The internal library information gives a picture of the present and past use of the library. This information includes

- the number of patrons,

- the number of people who visit the library,

- the circulation and interlibrary loan statistics,

- reference statistics (both in person and by telephone or online),

- computer usage statistics, and

- program statistics.

When possible, these statistics should be divided by age and any other patron characteristics such as gender or language preferred that can be retrieved from the circulation information. Reference use, computer usage, and program statistics may be available by age and so forth. These internal library statistics are regularly collected and can be compared with statistics collected in past years. The internal library information should also include what kinds of programs and services are offered, library outreach efforts, major library achievements, and a description of the collection.

Community Profile

The external community information is a view of both the population and the environment of the community. It gives a broader view of who lives in the community by age, gender, education level, income, ethnicity, and so forth, and how that compares with who uses the library. Are there also patrons who use the library regularly who are not members of the community? The environment includes climate, housing, retail areas, recreational opportunities, and whether there are any geographic impediments such as a river or a major highway. To develop a community profile, a great deal of data must be collected that includes the U.S. census data about the community (ages of local residents, ethnic background, education levels, income levels, etc.). Good sources of census information are https://data.census.gov and the American Community Survey. Local data may also be available that has been collected by the city, county, or state. Other sources of information are local business reports such as from the chamber of commerce, information from a local or county planning office, information from local newspapers, information on community services provided, and information on local government, local organizations, and community groups. It will also be important to identify community trends and interests. Are there local sports teams, local education-oriented groups, strong religious groups, and groups organized by area of interest? This information can be compared with earlier internal and external data to see if there are changes in the use of the library, in the makeup of the community, and in what is happening locally. Are there more or less people in poverty? Has the unemployment rate gone down or up? What ages in the population are expanding? Doing this evaluation will point out changes the library needs to make and unexpressed information needs. Community trends should also be noted. What kinds of technology do local patrons use? How is the economy affecting the residents? How are the demographics changing? What social media is popular?

Mission Statement and Vision Statement

Strategic plans should begin with strategic thinking and by evaluating the library's mission and vision statements. If it does not exist, the first step can be to develop a mission statement. The library's mission statement should focus on its patrons and the services it provides for them now. It should be action oriented. The mission statement focuses on the now and describes the library's commitments to its patrons and to its community in just a few words. Mission statements reflect how the public library sees its current role. They use action verbs such as advances, guides, provides, empowers, and enriches. They articulate the movement of the library forward as it serves its patrons and communicate how the library differentiates itself from other local groups and institutions. It is important that the library staff also understands the mission statement.

The vision statement focuses on the future—what the library wants to be—and tends to be more inspirational and exciting. It is written in the present tense. It is less factual and more visionary. It is positive and shows that the library is looking forward toward the future.

Some examples of mission and vision statements follow. These examples show how the mission statement and vision statement are linked, describing both the present and the future.

Free Library of Philadelphia. *Mission:* The mission of the Free Library of Philadelphia is to advance literacy, guide learning, and inspire curiosity. *Vision:* Its vision is to build an enlightened community devoted to lifelong learning.

Queens Public Library. *Mission:* Queens Library transforms lives by cultivating personal and intellectual growth and by building strong communities. *Vision:* Our vision is a vibrant, informed, cohesive, and empowered society.

Denver Public Library. *Mission:* Together, we create welcoming spaces where all are free to explore and connect. *Vision:* A strong community where everyone thrives.

Needs Assessment

The library must first administer a needs assessment to determine if it is serving the needs of the community and what new services it might want to provide and if there are services that are no longer needed. Needs assessments can be conducted in a variety of ways: by outside consultants, volunteers, or library staff. Some possible tools to use to collect data are surveys, focus groups, interviews, and community forums. Surveys can be useful since they provide feedback from a large number of library patrons and nonpatrons at fairly low cost. They can be conducted in person, by telephone, by mail, or online. With surveys it is important to test them to be sure the questions are receiving the response wanted. It is a good idea to have someone who knows how to frame questions for a survey review the draft of the survey. Testing it out is also a good idea since it is possible to see if the responses are the right ones or if the question has been misunderstood.

- In-person surveys can be administered in the library. Someone must hand out the surveys to the patrons and receive them when they have been completed.

- Surveys by telephone are harder to administer now because of answering machines, so the survey may not return useful results.

- Surveys by mail are fairly expensive since the postage rate has increased. But if residents fill them out surveys by mail can be useful and not intrusive.

- Online surveys are one of the best ways to collect information. It is less costly since it can be made available on the library's website or sent out from Survey Monkey or other online survey software. If there are ways to send out the survey beyond library users, nonusers can be encouraged to respond.

Focus groups are useful because they provide a way to get more specific information from a selected group of patrons about community needs. Each focus group can have participants who represent a different group or area of interest. They are more time consuming because people have to be carefully chosen for the focus groups and the results have to be taped and transcribed. There could be a focus group just for the staff. The focus groups will also need a trained facilitator who could be a staff member with some focus group training.

Interviews can be used as a way to get information from specific people. They can be useful particularly if the library interviews key people in the community. It is also a chance to interview nonusers. But once again, interviews are more costly and require both preparation time and time for the interview to be transcribed from the notes taken. Interviews generally last thirty minutes.

Community forums are an excellent way to get a great deal of community feedback. They can be held in the library or at other neighborhood locations. This gives many patrons and especially nonpatrons an opportunity to contribute their ideas about the library. The library should have a staff member in charge of these community forums since they must be organized in advance, and the information gathered should be written up for future use.

Many recommend that as part of the strategic plan development doing a SWOT study. SWOT stands for strengths, weaknesses, opportunities, and threats. The reason for using SWOT is that it is important to reflect on the library's strengths (e.g., what the library does well) and its weaknesses (e.g., what the library can do better and maybe services no longer needed), which can be measured internally. The opportunities (e.g., where the library can benefit by taking advantage of something happening in the community) and the threats (e.g., services done by the library that are already being done by others) are external and may be beyond the control of the library. Strengths could be the staff or the quality of the collection. Weaknesses could be the lack of sufficient budget or the need for additional staff. Opportunities could be funding to add new formats to the collection or a new van for the library. Threats could be the lack of sufficient local funds for the library.

The alternative to SWOT is SOAR, which is based on appreciative inquiry. SOAR looks at strengths, opportunities, aspirations, and results. Strengths are what the organization does right, opportunities are challenges that are more positive than weaknesses, aspirations are what the organization aspires to do, and results or outcomes are ways to see we are on track to accomplish what we set out to do. SOAR also calls for a great deal of participation by stakeholders, including staff and patrons.

Another way to approach planning is scenario planning. Using the information gathered, alternative futures are written. These futures are based not necessarily on the past but on possibilities as to what will happen in the future. The idea of these scenarios is to think through them, thus better preparing the library for the future. As an example, they can involve the library's budget. How will the library deal with a serious budget cut as a result of the library's primary funding source having less money? Or what would the library do with more funding?

Analysis of the Results

From the results of the needs assessment the library can begin to establish priorities, and from the priorities will come the goals and objectives. This will form the basic strategic plan for the library. One way to organize the results is by subject based on the surveys, focus groups, interviews, and community forums. Begin by asking a series of questions such as the following:

- What issues come up often either positive or negative?

- What are areas where users agree that the library is doing well?

- What are areas where users are indicating that more can be done?

- Are there new areas that the library needs to develop?

Goals and Objectives

Goals and objectives are based on the study of the community and the library and the needs assessment. Many are confused as to what are goals and what are objectives. Goals are more general statements. They are written in positive language and should be ways to benefit the community. Objectives are more specific and are measurable and achievable. They are more short ranged than the goals. Libraries usually write action items for each objective so it is clear how the objectives will be met.

Think of goals, objectives, and actions in the following way:

Goals:

- Are general and not specific
- Discuss community benefits
- Show movement forward

Objectives:

- Are specific and measurable
- Are time specific
- Are short range

Actions:

- Are concrete tasks
- Show how tasks will be accomplished
- Identify who will be assigned each task

Goals and objectives should move the library forward. If the goals and objectives just repeat what the library is presently doing, they are of no use. The library may look perfect to many, but that is usually not the case. There are often many nonusers of libraries, and it is important to find out why these people do not use the library. In order to find this out, the community surveys will have to get out into the community to meet with nonusers. Looking at the results of SWOT is also a good thing to do. Sometimes looking at the weaknesses and threats will give the planning committee ideas for how to turn them into positives.

An example of goals and objectives from the Forsyth County (Georgia) Public Library's Strategic Plan, 2013–2018, is the result of input from the public and the staff. Each of these objectives lists activities to make it easier to evaluate the results.

1. Establish the library as a civic focal point and resource hub.
   a. Increase awareness of the library's programs, services, and resources.
   b. Increase the number of partnerships with Forsyth County organizations to enrich and expand community relationships.
   c. Promote the library as the first and best source of lifelong learning.

2. Develop relevant and inspiring collections that meet Forsyth County's evolving needs and expectations.
   a. Select and maintain high-quality popular and informational collections.
   b. Sustain a balance between traditional and electronic collections.
   c. Increase funding to support FCPL collections.

3. Provide a high-tech/high-touch approach to serving the community.
   a. Develop technology that makes accessing knowledge and ideas easy and intuitive.
   b. Make library facilities premier locations in Forsyth County.
   c. Provide personal, exceptional service.

4. Encourage and support all the library staff to be an engaged and energized workforce.
   a. Provide training to increase the proficiency of library staff in their job responsibilities.
   b. Foster an organizational culture of innovation and involvement.
   c. Help staff to readily adapt to change. (Beasley 2013, 25–26)

An example of just one of the goals and objectives of the Russell Library of Middletown, Connecticut, is the following. It states the objectives of the goal in clear terms that are easy to evaluate.

COMMUNITY LEADERSHIP

Goal:

We will become a leader in bridging the Middletown of today to the Middletown of tomorrow by forming structured partnerships that enable the Library to extend its reach and share its resources so that we all can provide enhanced benefits to the community.

Objectives:

1.1 Expand collaboration with not-for-profit community organizations to match their expertise and skills with the Library resources, and provide a cost-effective expansion of services.

1.2 Revisit cooperative opportunities with all schools in the community, both public and private, to engage a full range of students at the earliest age possible and continue to attract students to the Library through to graduation.

1.3 Partner with youth agencies to provide a richer set of resources for teens.

1.4 Look for opportunities to match the Library's resources, especially in the area of technology and job search, with local community service providers.

1.5 Form strategic partnerships with local business and business organizations to promote mutual interests.

1.6 Form advisory groups in the areas of programming, technology and operational efficiency and skilled, experienced community members to join in providing the Library with advice and information.

1.7 Enhance the Library's ability to communicate with all members of the community by developing a unifying message, social network communication channels and upgrading the website.

1.8 Invite all members of the community to unite in an annual series of events to identify and celebrate the community's values. (Gray and Meyers 2013, 327–28)

Action Plan

Implementation of the Strategic Plan/Action Plan

Once the strategic plan is in place, a staff member should be designated to supervise the implementation plan. The implementation plan is based on goals, objectives, and activities or actions outlined in the strategic plan. Each objective will have activities or actions that indicate how the objective is to be carried out. This can include who will be assigned to each action and what the time line is for completing the task. Whoever is in charge of implementing the strategic plan will want to begin with a staff meeting so that everyone understands what will be happening. Certainly much can change, even if the strategic plan is for three years, so the plan should be flexible enough to change if needed. Each objective needs to be examined to see if progress is being made; that is, how well the library is implementing each objective and what else needs to be done. Periodic reporting will help to document the progress on the strategic plan.

One approach would be to have a time line and put all the actions in it. Then when the planning/implementation committee meets, committee members will be able to see how much has been accomplished and what remains for this strategic plan. It is impossible to judge exactly how long certain actions will actually take since some of them may turn out to be more challenging than originally thought. For example, if the library decides to try to recruit new users for the library, especially from neighborhoods that have not traditionally used the library, this might take longer than planned. But the staff has to have an idea of how to implement the objectives and actions. That is, the actions must be integrated into part of their daily or weekly operations. If they need additional resources, then they must be provided. If the actions seem impossible, probably a change is needed.

Evaluating the Implementation of the Plan

An evaluation plan should be in place at the beginning of the strategic plan so the library can evaluate what it accomplished. Having measurable actions is one way to be certain that the evaluation is possible. There should be some quantitative and qualitative measures. This means that the quantitative measurements can probably come from the action items plus other statistics the library is collecting. The qualitative measurements will be developed based on the objectives and actions. They could be interviews, focus groups, surveys, or comments about the library from social media.

The Next Steps

Before another strategic plan is designed the library will want to take a step back and see how well they have done. New data will need to be collected so that any changes will be figured into the next strategic plan. This process is an important one for libraries. Planning is an important part of the development of the public library. It is easy to become complacent and just assume all is going well. That may or may not be the case. But always having a strategic plan in place and then developing a new one will keep everyone thinking ahead. The question will be "What do we need to do next?" Communities are changing, and the library must change with them.

Discussion Questions

1. What are some of the benefits of strategic planning for the library?

2. Do you recommend that the staff be involved in strategic planning, and, if so, how should they be involved?

Bibliography

American Community Survey. (n.d.). https://www.census.gov/programs-surveys/acs.

Beasley, Carla. 2013. "Forsyth County Public Library Strategic Planning, 2013–2018." *Georgia Library Quarterly* 50, no. 2 (Spring): 19–27.

Gray, Alan Kirk, and Arthur Meyers. 2013. "A Strategic Plan for Russell Library, Middletown, 2013–2017." *Public Library Quarterly* 32, no. 4 (October): 322–32.

Hall, Kate, and Kathy Parker. 2019. *The Public Library Director's Toolkit*. Chicago: American Library Association.

CHAPTER 3

LIBRARY ESTABLISHMENT, POLICIES, AND GOVERNANCE

- How are public libraries organized?
- Library policies
- Materials lending policy
- Collection development policies
- Patron behavior policy
- Meeting room policies
- Patron confidentiality policy
- Internet policy
- Displays, exhibits, and bulletin boards policy
- Gift policy
- Personnel policy
- Volunteer policy
- Boards of trustees
- Types of boards of trustees
- What do boards of trustees do?
- Relationship between the board of trustees and the library director

A public library is an organization that is shaped by what is needed in order to accomplish its mission, goals, and objectives. It is divided into units often by function but also by geography or type of customer. Usually the people who work for a public library all have job descriptions, so it is clear what they are assigned to do. There is an organization chart so everyone knows how units and positions are related. A public library works within a framework that provides direction as well as flexibility, and a public library is able to change and adjust as its community changes. As public libraries change, so does its organization. Some units in the library may expand and others may shrink. Timing can be very important. The library must know when it needs to change. Sometimes this is the result of new emphases in the library, and other times it is due to less interest in a particular unit.

How Are Public Libraries Organized?

Public libraries can be organized in many ways, but their establishment and the role of the board of trustees will follow state law.

- Public libraries can be a department of the local municipality. In this case the library is part of the local government and the library director reports to the mayor or city manager. These libraries also have a board of trustees that is more advisory. Libraries that are a department of the local municipality can participate in many services provided by the municipality, such as personnel services and ordering supplies and equipment. The budget for the library will be approved by the municipality after being reviewed by the board of trustees.

- Public libraries can be a school district library that is under the jurisdiction of a school district. They will also have a board of trustees. Often in this situation the local residents will approve the budget for the library at the same time as the school budget is approved.

- Public libraries can be organized as independent units that are funded either through private funds or a combination of private and public funds. Independent libraries do not report to any particular authority. They have a board of trustees and conduct their business in accordance with the laws of their state. If the library is organized in this way, it will have to carefully follow the state law and be aware of local and county laws that might apply to the library. This allows the library a lot of leeway but also means there is more responsibility.

- Public libraries can be members of a library system, such as a county library system. There may be a fee for belonging to the county library system, but then there are services provided to members such as a centralized circulation system, the ability to borrow from other libraries, and acquisition of books and media ordered and processed. They will also have a board of trustees.

All of these libraries can be just one unit or can be multiple units with a central library and branch libraries. Each state has its own laws. The laws usually cover the establishment of public libraries, the types of public libraries recognized, and the role of the boards of trustees. Three examples are Ohio, Colorado, and New York State.

In New York State there are four types of public libraries: municipal public libraries, school district public libraries, special legislative district public libraries, and association libraries.

In Colorado, municipal, county, and regional library authorities are recognized.

In Ohio, the following types of public libraries are recognized: association, county, county extension, municipal, school district, township, and regional library district.

Each state is slightly different and uses different words to describe the types of public libraries structures recognized.

Library Policies

Through a series of policies the library communicates its principles and priorities on many different parts of the library's operation. The staff and/or the director may draft policies, but the policies must be approved by the board of trustees. Policies cover every part of the library's work. Policies ensure uniformity in responding to specific issues and provide for a level playing field so that all patrons are treated equally. Policies start with an overall statement followed by procedures to provide needed step-by-step detail. It is important that policies are carefully written so they are clear and easy to explain and enforce. Policies cannot conflict with federal, state, or local law. Both the staff and patrons need to know what the library expects. Once adopted, the patrons should be made aware of all policies. Most libraries keep policies gathered in one place so they are easy to find. They are often available on the library's website. Policies should be stated in the positive if at all possible.

Policies make a library run better because everyone (the staff and patrons) knows what to expect. A policy sets up boundaries that articulate the general limits and directions and guard against differences in interpretation. External policies include materials lending policies, patron confidentiality policies, collection development policies, patron behavior policies, and meeting room use policies. Internal policies include personnel policies and policies about volunteers.

The ways policies are written and organized differ from library to library. Sometimes a great many items are included in one policy. Other times the same information is broken down into several policies. There is no right way to do this. But it is important that libraries have policies for the various parts of the library's work. Not having policies forces the staff to translate the information for each user. This can result in slightly different policies that may not be completely fair to the patrons.

RECOMMENDATIONS FOR LIBRARY POLICIES

1. Policies should be in line with the library's mission statement.

2. Policies should be in uniformity with the library's strategic plan.

3. Policies should not be in conflict with federal, state, or local laws.

4. Policies should not conflict with other library policies.

5. Policies should treat everyone equally.

6. Policies should be clear and easy to follow.

7. Policies should represent good library practices.

8. Policies should provide an overview of the issue and may be followed by procedures.

Materials Lending Policy

Materials lending policies are usually very detailed since there are a lot of different rules involved in loaning materials. It is important that all these rules are written down so there is uniformity in how the policy is administered. The following are some of the most important areas to include in a materials lending policy:

- How to apply for a library card

- Who is eligible for a library card—youth may have different rules from adults, and often nonresidents must pay for a card

- The length of the loan for different kinds of material such as books and videos

- The fines (if the library still charges fines) for overdue library materials

- Different fine schedules for adults and children

- Maximum fine limits for any one item

- How the library deals with lost library materials and damaged library materials

Collection Development Policies

Collection development policies cover what materials a library selects for its collection, including subjects acquired, the formats, and the age levels of the materials and the languages collected. For example, local history materials might be collected by the local historical society and not the public library. The policy will list the criteria used to select materials for the collection, which might include reviews and suggestions from patrons. It will also list the criteria for discarding materials from the collection. Most public libraries do not keep all materials forever, so it is important to state how these decisions are made. A collection development policy will discuss gift books and how they are handled by the library. It usually starts by stating that once books or other formats are given to the library, it is at the discretion of the library as to whether the materials are placed in the library collection or donated to others. The policy will state how the library will deal with books or other materials that are challenged by the library patrons following the guidelines of the American Library Association's Library Bill of Rights. There is usually a procedure that the library follows so it is clear that all points of view have been examined. (See the chapter on collections for a complete discussion of collection policies.)

Patron Behavior Policy

Patron behavior is an important policy for the library. It is important since the library staff and patrons need guidelines to define appropriate behavior. Staff members need to know what behavior is acceptable and unacceptable, and they need a written document to back them up. The following issues are usually addressed:

- Behaviors that are not appropriate in the library, such as ones that involve noise, food and drink, drugs, alcohol, smoking, animals in the library, and damaging of library property

- Behaviors in the library that are disruptive, threatening, abusive, bothersome, or unsafe

- Appropriate dress, such as if shoes must be worn

- Use of cell phones and other electronic devices

- Objects that could be unsafe, such as scooters, skateboards, roller blades, bicycles, and large carts

See the Code of Conduct policy of the New Haven Free Public Library at the end of the chapter.

Meeting Room Policies

The use of meeting rooms in libraries has become more important since many different groups are needing space to meet. It is important for the library to have a policy that is fair to all. Libraries can state

- that meetings must be open to the public,

- that no group can meet on a weekly basis, which will exclude certain groups but be more equitable,

- that certain hours are available for meetings,

- whether food and drink are allowed,

- whether fees can be charged, and

- how meetings can be advertised.

The following is the statement from the New Jersey Library Association:

> As limited public forums, NJLA supports the use of public spaces in libraries for a wide variety of activities. Libraries may limit certain services and resources to residents and cardholders, but should in all other respects welcome members of the public into their public spaces. A library may designate one or more rooms as public meeting spaces or meeting rooms, which may be reserved in advance. If it does so, the library should have policies governing the use of those spaces or rooms which are consistent with the library's mission. Such policies should provide for equitable access, be consistently applied, and be readily available to the public. (New Jersey Library Association 2014)

See the Toledo Lucas County Public Library Meeting Room Policy at the end of the chapter.

Patron Confidentiality Policy

Patron use and records confidentiality has become more important in the last few years as people worry about how information about library use will be used. The library must follow state law with regard to confidentiality. This usually involves assuring patrons that their use of the library and its materials will not be revealed to others. This policy might include the following:

- Stating the state's law on privacy of user records

- When user records can be disclosed, following state law, and what the procedures are for doing so

- What is protected, such as materials used, programs attended, and staff assistance

- Who in the library is responsible for ensuring that the confidentiality policy is implemented

Internet Policy

An internet policy often starts with explaining that the library is not responsible for the content of the internet. It will include the following:

- Prohibited behavior, such as using software and hardware inappropriately, should be stated.

- The American Library Association's (ALA) position on filters—"Internet Filtering: An Interpretation of the Library Bill of Rights." This position says that everyone should have equal access to the internet.

- If the library plans to apply for e-rate discounts, then the CIPA (Children's Internet Protection Act) guidelines apply. This means that minors under the age of seventeen must use a computer with a filter but that adults can ask to have access to the internet without the filters.

- The policy should include how patron's privacy and confidentiality will be protected. It is also important to warn patrons that the copyright laws applicable to internet.

Displays, Exhibits, and Bulletin Boards Policy

Everyone has an opinion about displays, exhibits, and bulletin boards so it is helpful to have a policy that provides guidance as to what is acceptable. This is a hard one to enforce. Here are some guidelines libraries can use:

- Procedures for requesting to post, display, or exhibit materials in the library

- Who gets priority for exhibits and displays

- Objective materials that present both sides of a controversial issue are preferred

- Usually, political campaign literature, legislative lobbying, religious proselytizing, and commercial advertising are not allowed

- All exhibits, displays, and postings must be approved

- There may be a time limit on how long exhibits and displays can be shown

See the Santa Cruz Display Policy at the end of the chapter.

Gift Policy

Gift policies must be very specific since users want to give many things even beyond books and other resources to the library. So libraries should be clear what they will accept and what they will be able to do in terms of a receipt for the gift. Some of the guidelines in gift policies are as follows:

- Once the library receives the gift, it is the library's right to decide on the disposition of the gift.

- The library will detail the conditions of gift acceptance.

- If the gift is a book or another library resource, it must meet the standards in the library's collection development policy.

- The library will describe how it will acknowledge the gift.

- The library will state that the value of the gift cannot be determined by the library. The user can get an outside appraisal if that is needed.

See the Santa Cruz Gift Policy at the end of the chapter.

Personnel Policy

Personnel policies are an important internal policy. If the library is part of a town or city government, the personnel policy for the municipality will govern the library staff. Also, if the staff is unionized, the union contract will govern the union staff and another policy will be developed for nonunion staff. But for many libraries none of the above apply; therefore, the library will develop a detailed personnel policy. The personnel policy will include work schedules; salary schedules or how salary raises are handled; benefits such as health insurance, vacation leave, sick leave, retirement benefits, and leaves of absence; performance evaluations; disciplinary action; and professional leave for conferences. (See more details in chapter 4.)

Volunteer Policy

Volunteers can be a major part of any public library. But it is important that their responsibilities are carefully outlined in an internal policy so they know what the library's responsibilities toward them are and what is expected of them. Having procedures for volunteers makes for a better working relationship. The following guidelines are useful in a volunteer policy:

- How volunteers contribute to the work of the library

- Who is eligible to be a library volunteer

- What volunteer opportunities are available

- How to apply

- The volunteers' responsibilities

- The library's responsibilities to volunteers

- Guidelines for the conduct of a volunteer when working for the library

Where to Find Sample Policies
The Library Development Office of the State of Colorado has provided a series of sample Colorado policies available at this URL: http://www.cde.state.co.us/cdelib/librarydevelopment/publiclibraries/Policies.

Boards of Trustees

The board of trustees is an important part of the public library's organization since it is a layperson group that reflects the community's view of the public library. Their responsibilities and duties vary depending on the organization of the public library. Board members can be either appointed or elected. There are many ways to gather community opinions on the public library, but the board of trustees is a starting point since they usually meet every month and have the best knowledge of the public library.

Types of Boards of Trustees

Boards of trustees may be administrative or advisory. If the library is independent of the municipality, the trustees will be administrative and will carry out the following duties:

- approving policies,

- approving the budget,

- helping in library planning,

- hiring the library director, and

- advocating for the library.

If the board of trustees is advisory, which is the case when the library is a department of the municipal or county government, it approves policies, engages in planning for the library, and advocates for the library. These different ways of organization have both advantages and disadvantages. If the library is independent of the municipality or county, it can move forward without consulting. If the library is a department of municipal or county government, it can take advantage of municipal or county services such as a personnel office and purchasing office.

Table 3.1. Comparison of administrative and advisory boards of trustees

Administrative Board of Trustees	Advisory Board of Trustees
Approves library policies	Approves library policies
Approves the budget	Provides input on budget needs
Participates in short- and long-range planning	Participates in short- and long-range planning
Hires the library director	Provides input when a library director is hired
Advocates for the library	Advocates for the library

The appointment of public library boards of trustees follows the laws of the state. This law, which is part of the state code or found elsewhere in state legislation, will state how many members the board of trustees should have, how they will be appointed, and the length of their term of service. The state code will usually indicate that meetings of the public library board of trustees are open to the public. Sometimes there are local regulations that apply to the public library. Boards of trustees have their own bylaws as well, which discuss how the board will operate, including

- the election of officers,

- the duties of each officer,

- board committees,

- terms and reappointments,

- how vacancies are filled,

- how bylaws are amended,

- the scheduling of meetings, and

- issues of conflict of interest.

There is usually a president, a vice president, a secretary, and a treasurer of the board. Sometimes the library director acts as the secretary of the board. The board may have standing committees or it may choose not to have standing committees, and the president will appoint an ad hoc committee when needed. Meetings of the board should be held on a regular basis. Most boards meet once a month. The board should be aware of any ethics violations, especially conflicts of interest.

Who are the members of the board of trustees? Ideally, the board of trustees represents different parts of the community. The board of trustees is usually appointed by a local official or elected by the community. The members of the board of trustees should preferably know their community—well, be knowledgeable about the library, its services, programs, and policies—and be interested in the library. Sometimes there are ad hoc members of the board, such as a representative of local government. Trustees should not be appointed for political reasons.

New members of the board of trustees will need an orientation so they understand their role and basic information about the library. Often orientation for new trustees is provided by a state library or a state library association in addition to the local orientation.

What Do Boards of Trustees Do?

Library Policies

Boards of trustees are responsible for approving library policies. Usually a library policy is drafted by the library director and sometimes the staff, but the final approval must go to the board. For example, the library might want to change the fine schedule for the library. It may want to increase the fines but not charge fines to those over seventy years of age. This must come to the board of trustees, which will examine it in relation to both the budget and community relations, and approve or reject the recommendation.

Financial Oversight

The board of trustees is responsible for financial oversight and control. They will receive an update of the financial situation of the library at each board meeting. The director and the staff will draft the annual budget, but the board of trustees must review it and make final recommendations. They are a good barometer as to how the community will accept an increase in the library budget and will want to develop an explanation as to why this is necessary. The president or other members of the board of trustees may be asked to speak at community meetings about the budget. The board should not only be interested in the current financial situation of the library but also be doing long-term financial planning for the library. This may mean, for example, fundraising for a particular project or developing a plan for funding an expansion of the library building.

Hiring the Library Director

The public library director is selected and hired by the board of trustees. When a public library director resigns or retires, it is up to the board of trustees to form a committee to interview prospective candidates and to make a recommendation to the board as a whole. This is a very important decision for the board since having the right person as director is key to running a good and efficient library. In addition to hiring the library director, the board of trustees will want to evaluate the performance of the library director on a regular basis and support the work of the library director.

Approving New Programs and Services

Programs and services in general are approved by the board of trustees. They may not be asked to approve each program or service. But the board and director have certainly discussed in a general way the kinds of programs and services that are needed and are appropriate for the community. It is expected that the director will discuss with them any new directions for programming or services.

Advocacy

Advocacy for the library is another important role for the board of trustees. The trustees should be out in the community talking about the library, telling people about the library's programs and services, promoting new directions in programs, identifying prospective partnerships and services, and discussing the potential and value of the library. The trustees can find out more about what the local residents want from the library and bring that information back to the library. The connections in the community of library board of trustees members are vital to the library.

Advocacy also involves getting to know key government officials; speaking to local, state, and federal government officials; and inviting them to library events. This will require that the trustees are knowledgeable about issues of interest to the library, such as privacy and intellectual freedom.

Planning

Trustees should be involved in planning the future of the library, both short term and long term, including future needs for increased funding and for leadership succession. It could involve working with the director to plan a community engagement effort, identifying community priorities and planning how the library can meet them, and working with local government to be sure the library's plans mesh with those of local government.

Meetings

Board of trustee meetings should be carefully planned by the president of the board and the library director. Information the board will need for its meeting should be available in advance of the meeting. It is important that the board of trustees members feel their time at the board meetings is well spent.

Learning about State and National Library Issues

Members of the board of trustees should be encouraged to find out about state and national library development. Selected trustees may want to attend state or national library conferences and report back on interesting new trends. In the ALA, there is a division, United for Libraries (Trustees, Friends, Foundations), that presents programs at ALA meetings and provides training videos for trustees that can be shown at their meetings. Many states have their own trustee organization. By having trustees attend state and national meetings they can learn about library issues such as intellectual freedom.

Relationship between the Board of Trustees and the Library Director

The relationship between the director and the board of trustees is very important to the smooth running of the library. It must be clear to the board of trustees what their responsibilities are and what the responsibilities of the director are. The oversight of the library—its policies, finances, and building—is the responsibility of the board of trustees. The director of the library is responsible for the day-to-day operation of the library. The director is responsible for keeping the board up to date with information about the library—both library activities and library problems. It serves the director well to maintain good relations with the board of trustees and to call on the skills and interests of board members who can be useful in providing information. If a board member has a question about some part of the library operation or about a staff member, the board member should consult with the library

Table 3.2. Comparison of board of trustees and director responsibilities

Responsibilities of the Board of Trustees	Responsibilities of the Library Director
Approve new library policies	Draft and recommend new library policies
Review and approve the library budget	Develop the library budget
Hire and evaluate the library director	Administer the day-to-day library operation
Work with director and community to develop a long-range strategic plan	Work with trustees, staff, and community to develop a long-range strategic plan
Support building needs through fundraising	Bring building needs to the attention of the trustees
Advocate for the library	Provide information regularly on the library
Support efforts to pass state and national library legislation	Provide information on state and national library legislation

director. Even if the board member just wants statistics, the request should go to director and not to a staff member.

It is important to note that working with the board of trustees can take a great deal of the director's time, but the rewards from a good relationship are many. Strong community relationships are absolutely necessary in order to have a well-run library.

Discussion Questions

1. Why do libraries need policies? What happens when the library doesn't have policies?

2. What should a library director do to avoid conflict with the board of trustees over who does what?

Toledo Lucas County Public Library Meeting Room Policy

In keeping with its mission, Toledo Lucas County Public Library offers meeting room space to the public for educational, cultural, civic, and recreational purposes, subject to the rules outlined below. The rooms are available as a free community service when Library programs are not scheduled.

The Library supports and endorses the American Library Association's Library Bill of Rights, which states: "Libraries which maintain meeting spaces, exhibit space or other facilities open to the public should make them available on equal terms to all persons, regardless of their beliefs or affiliations."

The fact that an organization is permitted to meet at the Library does not constitute an endorsement of the organization's beliefs by the Library, its staff, its board of trustees, or the Lucas County Board of Commissioners.

1. All scheduled use must be open to the public.

2. An online reservation for Library meeting rooms must be completed before a group can use a room. The person requesting use of a meeting room will be held responsible for the order and conduct of the group and for any damage to Library property.

3. Groups may not fundraise, sell goods, solicit commercial services or future commercial services, charge admission, or ask for donations for their meetings/events held on Library premises. Meeting rooms are not available for profit making by organizations, businesses, private social gatherings or provision of health care services.

4. Each group is responsible for its own meeting publicity, which must not include the Library's information as a contact. Publicity must state that the meeting is not sponsored by the Toledo Lucas County Public Library.

5. Library audiovisual equipment is available only upon prior reservation, and to groups that have an experienced operator who makes arrangements in advance for training if needed. Equipment may vary by location.

6. The Library is not responsible for equipment, supplies or any other materials owned by a group and used in the Library. Each group is responsible for the set-up and running of its equipment.

7. Groups wishing to serve light refreshments may do so. Be prepared to supply your own equipment and utensils. Please note that groups using the Library meeting rooms are responsible for clean-up. Alcoholic beverages are not permitted on Library premises.

8. The group using the room may be responsible for setting up tables and chairs.

9. Young children accompanying adult users of the meeting room shall not be left unattended in the Library. Minors are not permitted to use meeting rooms without adult supervision.

10. The Library reserves the right to limit the number and time length of reservations made by individuals, groups or organizations in order that all have a fair opportunity to use the meeting rooms.

11. Groups holding reservations are requested to notify the Library of any cancellation at the earliest possible date in order to free the room for use by others. Groups failing to give notice of

cancellation twice in succession may be denied future use of meeting rooms.

12. Meeting facilities are available only during the hours the agency is open to the public. Reservations cannot extend later than 15 minutes prior to the agency closing time.

13. The Library will approve and schedule only those meetings that will not disturb other Library activities. The Library reserves the right to withdraw permission for use when conditions warrant such action and to stop meetings that interfere with the normal operation of the Library.

14. Failure to comply with these guidelines may result in the loss of future meeting room use. Concerns or questions about these guidelines should be referred to the agency manager or the appropriate administrator of Library locations.

15. All groups and individuals using the Library's meeting rooms must adhere to the Expectations of Behavior Policy.

Approved by the Board of Trustees—October 2015

New Haven Free Public Library (Connecticut) Code of Conduct and Suspension Policy

The New Haven Free Public Library's Code of Conduct and Suspension Policy protect first and foremost the rights and safety of library users and staff. They are also intended to preserve and protect the library's property, its collections and facilities and ensure the library is used for its intended purposes.

Please follow all posted library policies and official notices. The following is prohibited and repeated infractions will result in suspension of library privileges:

1. Entering the library without shirt or shoes; visitors must be appropriately clothed at all times.

2. Talking in loud tones.

3. Using audio devices in a manner that disrupts others.

4. Sleeping in the library.

5. Alcoholic beverages are strictly prohibited. Non-alcoholic beverages are allowed in covered, spill-proof containers only. Consumption of food in the building and possession of open food or beverages is not permitted, except in designated areas.

6. Unacceptable personal hygiene or other strong, pervasive odors that present a nuisance to patrons and staff.

7. Impeding ingress or egress to and from the building; aisles, walkways and doors must be clear at all times.

8. Loitering or smoking, including e-cigarettes, on library property.

9. Furniture must be used appropriately and may not be moved without prior staff approval.

10. Violating the Visitor Guidelines for Personal Belongings.

11. Using computers and the internet in inappropriate ways. Users must comply with the library's Internet Access and Wireless Policies.

12. Parents/caregivers must be in compliance with the Unattended Children Policy.

13. Bringing animals other than service animals into the library.

14. Selling or soliciting without prior library approval.

The following will result in immediate suspension of library privileges:

1. Damaging or defacing library property, including altering or damaging set-up of computer equipment or software.

2. Exposing others to health hazards (e.g., lice, infectious diseases, etc.).

3. Entering the library intoxicated; consumption of alcohol or other intoxicants in the building or on library property.

4. Harassing patrons or library personnel in any physical manner; or by using abusive, obscene, personally offensive or confrontational language.

5. Fighting in the library.

6. Any act that violates the City's Violence in the Workplace Policy.

7. Any illegal acts or conduct in violation of Federal, State or City law, ordinance, regulation or other Library Policy.

Those persons who violate these rules will be asked to leave. Those refusing to leave when asked are subject to arrest under trespass laws of Chapter 952, Sec. 53a-107, General Statutes of Connecticut.

Approved by the NHFPL Board of Directors, May 22, 2018

Santa Cruz Public Libraries Gift Policy

Santa Cruz Public Libraries (the Library) welcomes gifts of money (cash, securities, annuities, bequests, and trusts); materials; real, intellectual, or personal property; works of art for public display; and gifts in kind. Financial gifts to the Library are treated as revenue over and above the operating budget, and shall be used solely for the enhancement of basic library services, programs, materials, or facilities.

Gifts in value up to $25,000 are the delegated management responsibility of the Director of Libraries, who will make decisions regarding gift acceptance and disposition with the exception of gifts received under the Library Naming Policy. The Library retains the right to refuse any gift, and to make all decisions regarding the processing, use, placement, access, storage, retention, sale, donation, or disposition of any gift.

Gifts made unconditionally and without restrictions are preferred. Gifts with conditions requested by the donor shall be approved on a case-by-case basis by the Director of Libraries.

Ownership of gifts resides with the Library unless otherwise specified in a conditional agreement or if the gift is capital in function. Gifts of funding for capital changes to library facilities will be appropriated to and managed by the Jurisdiction.

Gift acceptance will be based on consideration of criteria including

- utility of gift toward Library strategic goals and objectives
- conditions placed on gift acceptance

- long-term maintenance obligation

- correlation with Collection Development Policy (for materials)

- jurisdiction capital campaign needs

- available space

- effect on future giving

Contracts are required when conditional gifts are given. Contracts associated with conditional gifts will be managed by the Friends of the Santa Cruz Public Libraries (the Friends) and signed by the Director of Libraries. When appropriate, the Library shall seek the advice of legal counsel in matters relating to the acceptance of gifts with conditions. If a gift condition is related to naming, please see the Library Naming Policy.

Copyright ownership of any gift donated shall be transferred to the Library so that the Library may make unrestricted use of the materials. Donors may wish to consult with legal counsel before transfer of copyright ownership.

Gifts will be received by the Friends, a 501(c)(3) non-profit organization whose purpose is to support the Library's strategic objectives, programs, and services through fundraising and advocacy. If a donor feels strongly that a gift must go directly to the Library, it will be accepted based on criteria stated herein. Gifts and gift monies will be held, invested, and allocated to the Library.

The Friends will acknowledge all accepted gifts in writing and will specify the type, quantity, and condition of the gift for the donor's records. Determination of monetary value of donations for donor income tax purposes will not be affixed by the Library. The Friends will follow non-profit laws and regulations regarding acknowledgement of all gifts.

Gift related record-keeping, and communication with donors related to gifts and ongoing gift management, is the responsibility of the Friends in consultation with the Director of Libraries. A record of all donations will be retained for seven years from date of acceptance, or for the duration of the contracted gift agreement.

Donors are granted the same right to access and use of their donation and the Library as other members of the public; unique or special access rights are not provided. The Library will not accept any gift that would result in placing a material obligation or lien upon the Library's operating budget.

The Library will provide the Joint Powers Authority Board with a quarterly gifts received report.

Approved: 8/20/17

Santa Cruz Public Libraries Display Policy: Bulletin Boards, Display Cases, and Wall-Mounted Exhibits

Policy Statement

In the context of its mission to enhance Santa Cruz County's quality of life by providing vibrant physical and virtual public spaces where people connect, discover, and engage the mind, the Library System makes available for community use display cases, bulletin boards, and other space for conveying information or publicizing events. The following rules govern the type and manner in which materials may be displayed.

Bulletin Boards

Bulletin Boards in public areas may be used to publicize cultural events and programs of community interest.

Notices about political candidates, religious services, or private enterprises may not be posted.

All materials must be submitted to the branch service desk for posting and approval.

Branches using digital signage may require posted notices to be received in or converted to electronic format for posting.

Display Cases

Use of Display Cases is reserved for individuals, non-profit and not-for-profit groups only.

Groups or individuals may reserve space in display cases on a first-come, first-served basis, by making arrangements in advance with the Branch Manager or her/his designee.

Generally, only one display per year per individual/organization may be booked at any one Branch.

Displays are for one calendar month.

Displays must be of interest to some segment of the community. They may not advocate the election of any candidate for political office. They may concern an issue of current political interest. It is understood that the opinions expressed in the display do not represent those of the Library System, its staff, or the Library Joint Powers Authority Board and signs stating this are posted at each Display Case.

The Library System will endeavor to make display space available to groups representing all sides of issues. It reserves the right to schedule displays on the first-come, first-served basis cited in Number 2 above. For displays regarding issues of current public debate, it also reserves the right to facilitate public comment on the issue via a binder in which people are invited to write their comments.

Each display must contain a sign indicating the name of the sponsoring group or individual. The sponsor may also post a sign listing its address and phone number so that interested members may contact the sponsor directly.

No work of art, craft, or artifact displayed may be priced for sale. The artist or sponsor of the display may post a sign within the display case stating that her/his business card is available at the service desk.

The Library System has no insurance covering the contents of display cases or other exhibits. If the sponsoring group or individual is concerned about insurance, it must make independent arrangements.

The group or individual must follow all rules regarding installation and de-installation established by the Branch at which the display is mounted. Groups or individuals sponsoring displays must sign a Display Reservation Form provided by the Library System stating the proposed content of the display and attesting that they understand the rules and policies governing displays.

Branch Managers or the Director of Libraries reserve the right to remove any display whose content does not reflect that stated in the Display Reservation Form.

Library reserves the right to remove displays after the month display period has ended.

Wall-Mounted Exhibits

All the strictures listed above apply to wall-mounted exhibits.

The Library System reserves the right to specify and limit the space in which wall-mounted exhibits are displayed.

The Library System reserves the right to form partnerships with Santa Cruz County arts organizations to select, coordinate, and manage the hanging of art exhibits.

Adopted by the Library Joint Powers Board September 10, 2001.
Rev. 08/24/01 Rev. 09/12/11 Rev. 09/08/14

Bibliography

Hall, Kate, and Kathy Parker. 2019. *The Public Library Director's Toolkit*. Chicago: American Library Association.

New Jersey Library Association (NJLA). 2014. "NJLA Statement of Meeting Room Policies." https://njla.org.

Pearlmutter, Jane, and Paul Nelson. 2012. *Small Public Library Management*. Chicago: American Library Association.

Prentice, Ann E. 2011. *Public Libraries in the 21st Century*. Santa Barbara, CA: Libraries Unlimited.

ORGANIZATION AND STAFFING

- Organization of public libraries
- Organization charts
- Staffing
- Job descriptions
- Competencies needed
- Professional staff
- Support staff
- Part-time staff
- Pages
- Volunteers
- Personnel policies
- Performance evaluations and disciplinary actions
- Training and professional development
- Management of staff

Organization of Public Libraries

Public libraries are shaped by what is needed in order to accomplish the mission, goals, and objectives of the organization. A public library is divided into units, often by function but possibly by geography or type of customer. Usually the people who work for an organization all have job descriptions, so it is clear what they are assigned to do. There is a chain of command so everyone knows who makes the decisions. A public library works within a framework that provides direction but also flexibility. Public libraries have to be able to change and adjust as their community changes. As public libraries change, so must their organization. Some units in the library may expand, and others may get smaller. Timing can be very important. The library must know when it needs to change. Sometimes this is the result of new emphases in the library, while other times it is due to less interest in a particular unit. Working on a new strategic plan is often a good time to examine the library's structure and make needed changes.

At the beginning the public library may have a few units or departments such as a circulation department, a reference department, a children's services department, a technical service department (acquisitions and cataloging), and an administration department. But as the library grows and expands there may be a need for more units or departments, such as a young adult services department, a media center, an outreach department, a technology department, a human resources department, and a business department. The library's organization must be large enough to accommodate all the functions of the library but not so specialized that responsibilities overlap. If there are too many staff in one department, it may be hard to manage them.

The library may be divided by function, location, format, or type of customer. Sometimes it is a mix of more than one type of department. For example, the library may have a reference department (function), a children's department (type of customer), a media department (type of format), and a circulation department (function). Each position in each department will have a job description. Some positions will have line responsibility, which means they have the authority to carry out orders, while others will be staff positions, which have the ability to provide advisory assistance but not direct authority. The librarian in charge of a branch will have a line position, whereas a staff member who plans programs will have a staff position.

Organization Charts

Looking at an organization chart is a good way to analyze how the library is arranged. It is important that the various tasks are organized so that it is clear who does what. With the organization chart you can see how positions relate to each other. You can see if a particular area has an overall supervisor and then someone in charge of a sub area. You can also see how many people report to a supervisor and whether that is too many for one person to handle. This is called the span of control. Organization charts can be arranged in many ways, but many will be arranged by function, such as circulation, public service, and technical service or a mix of function and geography if the public library has branches. The organization chart presents a formal view of the organization and indicates the reporting structure, which flows from the top down and outward. If there is a solid line on the organization chart, there is a direct line of authority. If there is a broken line, it is a staff office with no direct line of authority. Examples of staff offices are the business office and the human resources office. The organization chart cannot account for all of the ways staff need to work together, so a more informal structure emerges. One is not necessarily right and the other wrong. Staff members need to work across organizational lines to accomplish projects. For example, the young adult and children's staff might work together on a project.

The Aurora Public Library figure is an example of an organization chart for a library with two branches so there are units representing services to the whole library, such as maintenance, automated services, a computer network, and a unit for each branch. All units report to the director except the three services in the main library, adult services, children's services, and circulation services, which report to the head of the main library.

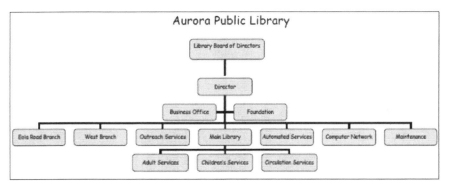

Figure 4.1.   Aurora (Illinois) Public Library District organization chart. *Aurora Public Library District, Illinois.*

Library organization charts change as the library adds branches. Sometimes there is a staff member who supervises the branches.

The Ocean County Library figure shows an example of a library system with many branches.

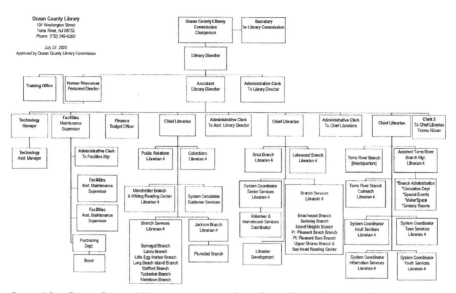

Figure 4.2.   Ocean County Library organization chart. *Ocean County Library, New Jersey.*

Staffing

Staffing in a public library has undergone many changes in the past few decades. As the work of the library becomes more diverse, the need for staff with a wider variety of competencies and skills has grown. The Public Library Data Service Report for 2017 shows that the staffing head counts in libraries has been relatively static over the past five years, although staff expenditure per capita has slightly increased (about 2–3 percent). "The average percentage of MLS librarians has increased at a rate of 0.71 percent. The average percentage of non-MLS librarians has increased faster (3.50 percent), offset by declines in other staff (–2.30 percent)" (Reid 2017). The technology used in libraries has grown tremendously so that staff members must be hired who have the background and training to maintain computer systems and who may or may not be librarians. This can include both ILSs (integrated library systems) that support the circulation and acquisitions work as well as individual computers used by the public. On the other hand, the library must do more marketing to call attention to its services and programming. Sometimes the best person for this position is not a librarian but rather someone with experience in public relations and marketing. When a library sets up a foundation, it needs someone with a background in foundation work or related work, and this person may not be a librarian. Many libraries hire full- or part-time social workers to assist them with patron problems such as the homeless and people with mental health issues that are beyond the skills of librarians. Many people with a wide assortment of issues are attracted to libraries and need immediate assistance.

A large city library has to find ways to be part of a neighborhood and to meet local community needs. At the Free Library of Philadelphia two community organizers were hired for each of their regions. These community organizers help with community engagement and outreach, work with local community organizations, and even go house to house telling people about the library and its services. The library also has two social workers who work throughout the library system.

A good time to review the staffing is after a planning process is completed. The planning process may reveal needs that require staff members with different skills. It may mean adding staff members or maybe just retraining the staff currently at the library. Here are some questions to ask:

- Can the work process be streamlined?

- Is this the best use of available staff?

- Do we need more staff?

- Can support staff handle a job done by a library professional?

- What data is needed to support staff changes?

Positions that were once thought to be the work of library professionals are now being performed by other staff in the library. For example, librarians once did a great deal of programming. But now other staff members often plan and provide programming. Librarians used to provide a great deal of public training sessions, but now many others are involved in this training. Librarians used to provide reference service. They still do, but others in the library have often been trained to provide first-level reference services such as directing users to the correct area of the library to find what they need or answering simple questions.

Staffing in general has changed. While the need for more technology staff has grown, the need for technical service staff (acquisitions and cataloging) has diminished. Libraries once cataloged and processed their books in-house, but now they can order their books online already cataloged and processed from a vendor or they can get the cataloging information from a vendor so that a clerical staff member can add the information to the book or other resource and to the online catalog.

The largest percentage (60–80 percent) of a public library's budget goes for personnel costs (salaries and benefits). It is important that personnel work is carried out in an organized manner since so much of the budget is used for this purpose. The staff is the library's most valuable asset. There are several categories of paid staff in a public library: professional staff, support staff, part-time staff, and pages. If a public library is small, there will be a few in each category, whereas if a public library is large, there will be many more staff members in each category and there may be other categories.

Job Descriptions

Job descriptions are very important, and everyone should have a job description, even part-time staff. Some job descriptions will be more specific and some will be more general. Job descriptions should include an account of the work, duties, and responsibilities of the position, education requirements, experience requirements, special skills required, the benefits package, and salary range. Libraries often forget to revise job descriptions. Job descriptions should be reviewed frequently and updated if necessary. There is an example of a job description following the discussion questions at the end of this chapter.

Competencies Needed

The need for new competencies is apparent in this changing world. Some competencies/skills are needed by everyone, regardless of the person's job title or job description. Here are some of the universal competencies/skills:

- Customer-service oriented

- Flexibility

- Adaptability

- Ability to use computers and other related technologies

- Multicultural understanding

- Appreciation of diversity

- Negotiation skills

- Commitment to intellectual freedom

- Ability to handle basic budgeting

- Basic understanding of statistics

This list provides an understanding as to how the world and the communities have changed and is a mix of soft skills and more technological skills. Staff members may not arrive at a library with all of these skills, but as long as they are willing to learn, the library will welcome them.

Professional Staff

The professional staff label sometimes only includes staff members with a master's degree—an MLIS, MLS, or other library degree. But as libraries are changing and staff members are hired with other advanced degrees such as information technology degrees, business management degrees, and marketing degrees, these individuals should be included in the professional staff category. Professional staff members play a different role than they previously played in many libraries. This is because, as previously stated, some tasks have gone to other staff members. Professional staff members usually perform supervisory duties and make decisions about the development of programs and services, as well as carry out other duties depending on the size of the library and the department in which they work.

Support Staff

The support staff performs many tasks in a library. There may be more than one level of support staff. The support staff often performs duties associated with keeping the website up to date and working with the ILS, which includes the circulation system and the online catalog, supporting computers for patron use, and supporting the audiovisual equipment in the library. Other support staff members may work at the circulation desk interacting with the public, answering questions people pose, or work in technical services preparing library materials for circulation. Many support staff members are local residents hired to work in the library.

Part-Time Staff

The part-time staff could be either professional or support staff. Many libraries do not have enough funds to hire all their staff on a full-time basis, so some of their staff members work part time, often 15–20 hours a week. Part-time staff members may later be promoted to a full-time position when one is available.

Pages

Libraries have traditionally hired students to shelve books and other library resources and perform related tasks. They work a few hours a week and are assigned a variety of duties. Pages can learn about the library through their work, and some go on to gain a library degree and become professional staff.

Volunteers

Many libraries use volunteers to work on specific projects. This is particularly useful in a small library that may not be able to hire enough staff for all its work. There should be a policy specifically about volunteers so it is clear what is expected of volunteers. When volunteers are hired, the library should have an agreement with them as to the number of hours they will work, their work schedule, and to whom the volunteer reports.

Personnel Policies

A good way to examine staffing is to look at what is included in a personnel policy. Libraries need a personnel policy with all procedures and benefits carefully spelled out. Everyone needs to know what to expect, and it should be the same for everyone. Sometimes personnel policies are guided by a union agreement and sometimes by civil service. But many libraries develop their own policies.

Hiring Procedures

Hiring procedures should be described in a personnel policy. The staffs need to know there is a level playing field. If the library is under civil service, this will dictate how new staff members are hired. It might include both a test and an interview. If the library is part of a union, once again procedures will be in place as to how hiring takes place. Many smaller libraries are under neither civil service nor a union. Here it is important that procedures are in place for hiring. It might include where the job is advertised and if there are any requirements besides an interview. Sometimes for a few jobs there is a test to see if the person can do the work required, such as for a job that requires lifting heavy boxes or a job that requires certain basic knowledge of computers or computer programs.

There is often a probationary period for new staff members. The newly hired staff members should be aware of this probationary period. It might be, for example, six months after which the staff member's work will be reviewed. During this probationary period, the new staff member should be mentored so they know what is expected of them.

Salaries

Employees need to know what the salary ranges are for the various job classifications in the library. It is important to state whether salary increases are for the most part automatic, such as a percentage increase for all the staff as determined by the board of trustees, or subject to an annual performance review.

Benefits

Libraries may offer a small or wider range of benefits to their staff depending on the size of the library and the library's budget. Possible benefits are listed below:

Health Insurance

Health insurance is of great importance to the staff, so it is important to tell them what coverage the library provides, what it includes, and whether it includes the family. Sometimes the library will provide a certain level of coverage, and staff members who want more can pay the difference.

Pension Plans

Libraries should provide pension plans if at all possible. Many staff members will not stay long enough to take advantage of a pension. But if they are in a standard plan, they may be able to continue it at their next place of employment.

Sick Leave

Most libraries allow a certain number of sick days or hours each year. It is important to let the staff know reasons sick leave may be taken and how to report sick leave.

Personal Days

Many libraries allow a few personal days each year that staff members can take at their discretion. They need to know how far in advance they must tell their supervisor that they plan to take a personal day and how to report these days.

Vacation Policy

Staff members need to know how many vacation days they are entitled to in a year. The library should spell out any rules about when vacation days can be taken and how much in advance they must be requested. Often the number of vacation days increases after a certain number of years at the library. Staff members need to know how long they must work at the library before they can take vacation days and whether they can carry over vacation days not taken to the next year.

Holiday Policy

Staff members should know whether they will be paid for holidays when the library is closed. If the library is open on certain holidays, the staff may be paid overtime for working those days or just be allowed to take another day off.

Work Schedules and Timekeeping

The staff should know how many hours a week is a regular work week. The staff should understand about the work schedules at the library. They need to know if their position has a particular schedule and whether it might vary from week to week. They need to know what to do if they want to request a change in their schedule.

Libraries have many different ways of keeping track of the hours the staff works. They may ask staff members to record the time they arrive and leave in some official way, such as punching in and out on a time clock. Or they may have a time sheet that each staff member fills out weekly. This will allow the library to know when the employee is taking a sick day, a personal day, a vacation day, and so forth.

The library often allows a short break in the morning and in the afternoon. It is important that the staff knows how much time is allowed for the break.

Leaves of Absence

Leaves of absence may be paid or unpaid. There will be a list of reasons for allowing paid leaves of absence, and there may also be an established procedure for paid and unpaid leaves of absence. Usually requests for leaves of absence must be in writing, stating the beginning and end dates and the reason for the request.

Resignations

The library will state the procedures for resignations. It can state how much in advance of the resignation the person must notify the library and whether the resignation should be in writing.

Retirements

The library will want to state how long in advance of a retirement the person must notify the library. The library will no doubt want the retirement information and date in writing. There will be paperwork that must be completed well in advance of the retirement date, and if a pension is involved, arrangements will need to be made for the pension to begin.

Grievances

If the library has a union or is under civil service, they may have a formal grievance procedure that the library must follow. But if not, the library should have a grievance policy in place so that it is prepared should the need arise. For example, the staff member can submit a grievance statement in writing and the human resource office will provide a response, or the staff member should talk to their supervisor or the director before submitting a grievance statement.

Performance Evaluations and Disciplinary Actions

Performance evaluations are important in order to provide staff members with information as to how they are doing. Performance evaluations may be needed for salary increases. But even if a performance evaluation is not needed for salary increases, performance evaluations should be done annually and should be a positive experience. At a performance evaluation the work of the staff member will be reviewed—both work completed and work yet to be completed. It is important to give staff members feedback and help them to develop and grow. It is a chance for a supervisor to have a conversation with the staff member. At this meeting the staff member and supervisor can set goals and objectives for the next year. The job description can also be reviewed to see if it needs to be updated. Often job responsibilities change and the job description remains the same. It is important that job descriptions reflect the work the person is doing.

Many libraries have opted for a progressive discipline approach to staff problems. In this approach, level 1 is a written notice from the supervisor indicating that there is a work-related problem. This might be in the form of an unsatisfactory performance evaluation. Level 2 will be a notice from human resources about the problem. Level 3 will be a hearing, and level 4 will be possible termination or suspension. This is so the employee will not be surprised that there is a problem to be solved. It is always hoped that once the employee is notified of the work-related problem, the problem will be corrected so that level 4 will be unnecessary.

See an example of a personnel policy at the end of the chapter.

Training and Professional Development

Training and professional development are important for all staff members. Hopefully there are some training opportunities offered close by that the staff can attend from time to time. They might be sponsored by the state library, the state library association, or a library system. Libraries should take advantage of these opportunities to send staff members to update them on library issues or to learn new skills.

Management of Staff

Staffing is continually changing in public libraries. More and more the lines between types of personnel are blurring as support staff take on roles once held by professional staff. Particularly in public service units, the public does not have a way to distinguish between a librarian and a support staff person. So public libraries realize that all staff members working at public service desks must have more training to be able to immediately serve patrons regardless of the question. To be sure, there is still a role for librarians since they will be a second level of service if more assistance is required and they will be participating in planning for the library.

Many libraries are trying to cross-train their staff—not only to perform several tasks but also to get a broader picture of the library. They are having their staff members work in teams, giving them opportunities to be more involved in the work of the library. Also, we see libraries moving staff members for long and short periods of time to other branches so they can see a different type of patron or a different way of doing the same tasks. This can be very refreshing and a good learning experience.

Employers should remain aware of what their employees want and how to retain them. Employees want opportunities to advance and grow in their work life. They want to feel valued and recognized for the work they do. They want to have opportunities for continuous learning. They want good communication in their workplace, and they want fair pay and benefits.

Discussion Questions

1. What are some ways a library director can stretch a small staff to still provide first-rate service?

2. What are the essential services that need the skills of a person with master of library science?

Example of a Job Description

Collection Development Librarian—Adult Specialist

Job summary:
Under the supervision of the adult services manager, employee is responsible for all aspects of collection development including related programming and outreach.

Description of duties of the position:

Identify, evaluate, and select appropriate materials according to the Collection Development Policy

Determine the strengths and weaknesses of existing collections and resources

Ascertain, analyze, and assess the needs of library patrons and staff

Design and perform appropriate and efficient procedures for materials selection

Identify, collect, and analyze appropriate data

Prepare reports and presentations relevant to department activities and responsibilities

Manage spending within established budgets in assigned collection areas

Manage the library's book groups including the Book Club Kits

Plan, coordinate, implement, and evaluate library programs to meet the objectives identified in library planning documents, and community needs, expressed or perceived

Represent the library on various community or professional bodies, as required or assigned

Qualifications:

Master's degree in library science with a minimum of two years collection development experience (public libraries preferred) or an equivalent combination of education and experience

Knowledge of current collection development principles and techniques and ability to apply them

Ability to plan, organize, and prioritize work activities in an efficient and streamlined manner

Familiarity with electronic methods and resources to analyze and evaluate collections

Effective oral and written communication and public relations skills

Experience with automated systems and electronic databases and resources

Willingness and ability to establish and maintain effective working relationships in a team environment

Personnel Policy

This Personnel Policy and any other policies or procedures of the Geneva Public Library (GPL or "the Library"), whether oral or written, are not contracts of employment and should not be relied on as such by any employee, as they may be changed at any time.

1. Civil Service

The employees of the Geneva Public Library are public employees and as such are subject to Civil Service. The Ontario County Department of Human Resources administers civil service for the Library, including reviewing job applications, scheduling and conducting civil service exams for competitive positions, and establishing and certifying candidate eligibility lists. The Library complies with New York State Civil Service Law and if a conflict occurs between this policy and the law, the law shall take precedence.

2. Organizational Structure

GPL is a non-profit organization, governed by a seven member Board of Trustees. The Trustees are responsible for hiring the Director. Within the guidelines of these policies and civil service regulations, the Director shall determine the recruitment, hiring, supervision, and termination procedures for all other staff.

3. Working Environment

3.1 Discrimination/Harassment

The Geneva Public Library provides a work environment that is free of illegal discrimination and harassment for both employees and non-employee service providers (vendors, consultants, contractors, subcontractors, and others) in conjunction with a contract. Any party who believes that he or she has encountered discrimination because of age, race, creed, color, national origin, sex, disability, genetic disposition or carrier status, or marital status in connection with his/her employment should discuss the problem with the Director.

A written complaint may be filed with the Director. If the complaint is against the Director, the complainant(s) may file a complaint with the Board of Trustees President directly.

The Director or Board of Trustees President shall make every effort to resolve the problem. If the problem is not resolved satisfactorily, the complainant may file a written complaint with the Board of Trustees, which shall hold a hearing within 30 days of receipt of the complaint and render a written decision within 20 days of the hearing. If the complainant is unsatisfied with the decision of the Board of Trustees, the complainant may file a formal complaint with the New York State or Federal Human Rights Commission.

Figure 4.3. Geneva Public Library Personnel Policy. *Geneva Public Library, New York.*

The Library maintains a Sexual Harassment Policy as part of our commitment to maintaining a workplace free from sexual harassment.

The Library complies with the Americans with Disabilities Act (ADA) of 1990 by taking steps to make its facilities barrier-free and accessible and making other adjustments to reasonably accommodate staff with disabilities.

3.2 Grievances
It is important to attempt to resolve differences or difficulties at the complaint level before they develop into grievances. Employees should first discuss problems with their supervisor and/or the Librarian II. If the difficulty cannot be satisfactorily resolved, or if the grievance involves the supervisor or Librarian II, then the Director should be contacted. Final problem resolution resides with the Director, except if the grievance involves the Director, when final resolution resides with the Board of Trustees.

3.3 Reporting Unethical, Improper, or Unlawful Behavior
The Library maintains a Whistleblower Policy that outlines a procedure for employees to report actions that they reasonably believe violates a law or regulation, or that constitutes fraudulent accounting or other practices.

3.4 Smoking
The Library is a smoke-free work area. No smoking is permitted on Library premises or within 100 ft. of an entrance.

3.5 Alcohol/Substance Abuse
No employee shall use, possess, or sell alcoholic beverages or illegal drugs on the Library grounds. The Library encourages employees with substance-abuse problems to seek treatment; however, seeking treatment for dependency does not exempt employees from disciplinary action.

This policy does not apply to legal beverages served at Library-sponsored events.

3.6 Guidelines for Compliance
The Library expects all employees to comply with all laws, policies and regulations applicable to the Library and to maintain confidentiality of Library records and transactions.

3.7 Computer/Software Use and Security
Library equipment including computer hardware and software are valuable assets. They should generally be used for Library business only, with the exceptions noted below. Employees may not copy or use Library purchased/leased software contrary to the provisions of any license agreement. Employees should follow computer maintenance, software updating procedures, and caution in opening email in order to avoid computer viruses which have the potential to cause damage to Library and system computer networks.

The Library provides Internet access and email to its employees to assist and facilitate business communications and work-related research. These services are for legitimate business use only in the course of an employee's assigned duties, with the exception that employees may access the Internet for non-business use on personal time, so long as all other provisions of this policy are followed. All materials, information, and software created, transmitted, downloaded or stored on the Library's computer system are the property of the Library and may be accessed by authorized personnel.

Figure 4.3. *(continued)*

Inappropriate computer use includes but is not limited to: transmitting obscene, harassing, offensive or unprofessional messages; accessing any site that is sexually or racially offensive or discriminatory; displaying, downloading or distributing any sexually explicit material; transmitting any confidential or proprietary Library information.

The Library reserves the right to monitor employee use of the email system. Employees should not consider their Internet usage or email communications to be private when using staff computers, software, or email accounts. Personal passwords are not an assurance of confidentiality, and the Internet itself is not secure.

Any software installed or other material downloaded on the Library's computers may be used only in ways consistent with the licenses and copyrights of the vendors, authors, or owners of the material.

3.8 Dress Code

Staff members must dress appropriately for their work assignment. Supervisors have the authority to determine whether particular outfits are inappropriate for the Library. Supervisors will discuss inappropriate dress with individual staff members.

Library employees are expected to be well groomed and neatly dressed. Each staff member should dress appropriately when working with the public to convey a positive and professional image of both oneself and of the Library, while remaining approachable to Library customers.

Unacceptable attire includes: bare midriffs; spaghetti straps; skirts or shorts shorter than just above knee length; torn, unhemmed, patched, or faded clothing; strapless tops, halter tops, muscle shirts, and low cut blouses.

Clothing or accessories with words or pictures which are political, abusive, demeaning, lewd, suggestive, offensive are prohibited. The Director reserves the right to deem any article of clothing or accessory to be inappropriate. On occasion, the Director may authorize exceptions to the dress code.

Casual attire is allowed for Library Pages, and on Fridays and Saturdays for all other employees in accordance with the above criteria. Some activities, such as cleaning days, outside activities, or craft projects, may call for variations from the dress code.

3.9 Social Media

Employees using social media for personal use may only do so during breaks, meal periods, and before or after scheduled work hours. Employees who choose to identify themselves as Library employees on their individual social media accounts are expected to, as best as possible, make it clear that their posted content does not reflect the views of the Library.

When using social media, employees are expected to abide by all applicable Library policies, including, but not limited to, policies concerning harassment, confidentiality, and use of technology. Employees may not post or display comments about patrons, coworkers, supervisors, or the Library which are obscene, vulgar, threatening, intimidating, harassing, discriminatory, or personal attacks.

Only authorized administrators can prepare and modify content for the Library's social media pages. No users shall use the Library social media accounts for commercial promotions, spamming, or political activity.

4. Schedule and Conditions of Operation

4.1 Holidays

Staff are paid for the following holidays on which the Library is closed:

- New Year's Day
- Martin Luther King Day
- President's Day
- Memorial Day
- Independence Day
- Labor Day
- Veterans Day
- Thanksgiving
- Black Friday
- Christmas Eve
- Christmas Day

Additional paid and unpaid holidays may be approved by the Board of Trustees.

Holidays falling on Sunday will be celebrated on Monday.

The Library closes at 5 p.m. on Thanksgiving Eve and New Year's Eve. These evenings are not paid holidays.

Part-time benefit-eligible employees are paid for holidays at the rate of 1/5 the hours of their average work week.

4.2 Weather and Emergency Closings

If the Library closes because of extreme weather conditions or emergency conditions, employees are paid in accordance with the Library's Emergency Closing Policy.

Employees scheduled to attend offsite functions that are canceled due to such conditions are required to cancel the offsite request and make up the time. If the Library is closed but an offsite function is still scheduled, the employee is not required to attend the function but may at their discretion. In instances where they elect to attend, they will not be paid for duplicate hours worked.

With the Director's or a supervisor's permission, time-off balances may be used to cover times when the Library is open but an employee believes traveling to or from work would endanger his or her safety.

4.3 Minimum Staffing Level

To be open, the Library must have each desk staffed and one additional employee in the building. In the event that staffing is below that level, the Director or a Supervisor should be notified. If additional staff cannot report to work, the building or individual floors will be closed. Modifications to the minimum staffing level must be approved by the Library Board.

4.4 Working Hours

In accordance with its status as Central Library, the Library is open at least an average of 55 hours a week, unless approved by the Board of Trustees due to emergency conditions or temporary closures related to construction or facility repairs.

The Director or his/her designee shall create a weekly work schedule. Occasionally, it may be necessary for employees to work hours different than his/her normal schedule to ensure the Library staffs each

Figure 4.3.   *(continued)*

information desk and adheres to the necessary number of open hours and. Providing work requirements are met and with approval from the Supervisor or Director, the daily work schedule may be shifted.

Employees are expected to adhere to their scheduled weekly work hour totals as much as it is possible given the Library's time reporting system and the requirements of working the information desks and closing the building. Employees may be asked, but are not required, to work more than their standard scheduled hours to meet the programming or operational needs of the Library. Such requests must come from the employee's supervisor or the Director and must be approved by the Director or his/her designee.

The Library provides unpaid 1/2 or 1 hour lunch or dinner breaks in accordance with New York State Labor Law. Staff working on Saturdays are entitled to a 15 minute paid break. Staff should refrain from working during their meal and break periods. In instances where a staff member is compelled to work while clocked out for a meal period, they should report the time worked to their supervisor so their time card can be amended. They should also make sure to then take at least a ½ hour meal period accounting for the time worked.

4.4.1 Working Remotely
The Library has provisions in place to allow staff to work remotely in order to ensure an efficient workplace and employee productivity during various situations, planned and unplanned, including long-term library closures.

Staff members may work remotely/from home under the following guidelines:

- The employee position must be conducive to working remotely
- All remote work requests must be approved by the Director or his/her designee
- The staff member must be able to demonstrate their ability to complete essential job duties while working remotely
- Remote working hours must comply with the staff member's regular working schedule; variations to that schedule must be approved by the Director or his/her designee
- Staff members must be available to the library by email, chat, and/or phone within a reasonable amount of time
- Staff members will not be reimbursed for phone calls, Internet access, equipment, or other expenses incurred.
- Staff members are responsible for providing the necessary technology and equipment to facilitate their work remotely unless the request to work remotely is prompted by the Library.
- If the Library requests a staff member work remotely, the staff member is responsible for communicating to the Library if they do not have the necessary technology or equipment to perform the task.
  - The Library will work with the staff member to either provide the technology or equipment or make a reasonable accommodation in the staff member's essential duties.

4.4.2 Other Offsite Meetings
All other requests to work offsite require prior approval from the requesting employee's supervisor or the Library Director.

4.5 Staying Home When Ill
The Library provides employees with paid time off and other benefits to compensate employees who are unable to work due to illness. During flu season and/or some other pandemic illness, it is critical that employees do not report to work while they are ill and/or experiencing influenza-like symptoms such as: fever, cough, sore throat, runny or stuffy nose, body aches, headache, chills, diarrhea, vomiting and

fatigue. The Centers for Disease Control and Prevention has recommended that people with influenza-like illness remain at home until at least 24 hours after they are free of fever (100 degrees F or 37.8 degrees C) or signs of a fever without the use of fever-reducing medications.

4.6 Staff Training

The Library conducts staff trainings during normal operating hours but may occasionally schedule training during closed hours. The Board of Trustees must approve trainings held during closed hours. When possible, the Library Director, or his/her designee in charge of scheduling the training, will provide at least one-month's notice to staff regarding the time of the event. Notice regarding the training shall detail the expectations for staff attendance at the training.

5. Compensation

All Library employees are paid every other week on Thursday. Direct deposit of wages, while not required, is strongly encouraged to minimize delays in payment and the Library's processing costs.

Non-exempt employees will be paid for hours worked. Hours worked over 40 per week will be paid at a rate of time and a half.

In the interest of recruiting and retaining qualified staff, the Board of Trustees shall annually review salary and wages to ensure that these recognize the contributions of all staff and are equitably established for exempt and non-exempt, full, and part-time staff alike; and that these are competitive with area libraries of comparable size, staffing, and organization.

6. Benefit Eligibility

To be eligible for the benefits provided by this policy, except for those benefits required by state and federal law, employees must maintain a work-schedule that averages at least ten hours a week, with the exception of Pages and Clerk Subs, who are not benefit-eligible under this policy. An employee's standard work schedules are to be approved by the Director and provided to employees in writing.

To receive full-time benefits as a designated full-time employee, an employee must work an average of 70 hours over each two week pay period. The average includes all approved paid time off, sick time, and offsite meeting requests, and unpaid leave.

The employee's supervisor and the Director maintain the right to monitor the average hours worked per pay period for each staff member. Employees are responsible for reviewing their own time cards and time off balances and immediately reporting any errors or concerns to their supervisor.

Supervisors are responsible for approving the time cards for all employees assigned to them in the organizational chart. In the case that a staff member has worked significantly over or under their approved scheduled hours for three pay periods in a calendar year, the Director may bring disciplinary notice against the employee subject to the provisions of Section 75 of New York State Civil Service Law. Supervisors reserve the right to modify submitted time off requests to correspond with an employee's scheduled hours and to correct overlaps in time worked or errors in the date/time of the request. Changes made to an employee's time card will be explained in the Library's time management system.

7. Time Off Benefits

7.1 Paid Time Off

Paid Time Off (PTO) gives benefit eligible employees paid time for vacation, personal, and sick time off requests.

Figure 4.3. *(continued)*

7.1.1 PTO Accrual

Exempt Employees and Librarians:

Years of employment at the Library	PTO Hours (Days) Accrued
Zero-Four	203 (29 days)
Five or More	238 (34 days)

Other Full-Time Employees:

Years of employment at the Library	PTO Hours (Days) Accrued
Zero-Four	133 (19 days)
Five-Nine	168 (24 days)
Ten or More	203 (29 days)

Part-Time Benefit Eligible Employees:

Years of employment at the Library	PTO Hours (Days) Accrued
Zero-Four	Employee's average weekly hours × 2.2*
Five or More	Employee's average weekly hours × 3.2*

*The average weekly hours are determined by the average work week of the employee in the previous calendar year or estimated average work week in the absence of a previous calendar year for new employees.

PTO hours will be awarded at the beginning of the calendar year. If an employee reaches five or ten years of employment, or receives an official increase in scheduled hours, as determined by a completed Schedule Change Request form, a prorated amount of the yearly PTO increase will be applied. The prorated calculation is rounded to the nearest start of a month.

New employees will be awarded their yearly PTO hours following two months of employment. The employee's PTO award will be prorated to the start of a month closest to the employee's official hire date.

(continued)

The employee's supervisor or the Director may approve the use of PTO for new employees in their first two months of employment. Such instances would result in an equivalent reduction in the amount awarded following two months of employment.

7.1.2 PTO Carryover

Up to 70 hours of paid-time-off may be carried over at the end of the year. If the employee has a PTO balance greater than 70 hours at the end of the year, the balance of PTO hours greater than 70 will be converted to sick time and added to the employee's sick time balance.

7.1.3 PTO Requests

In order to accommodate the scheduling and service needs of the Library, whenever possible, PTO requests for longer than one day require prior approval by the staff member's supervisor and at least two weeks notice before the first day of planned leave. Supervisors may approve requests with less notice at their discretion.

PTO requests shall not exceed three consecutive weeks in duration. Supervisors, in consultation with the Library Director and/or Board of Trustees reserve the right to approve exceptions to these restrictions as well as to deny requests to maintain the operational hours of the Library.

7.1.4 Payout for PTO Leave

Upon resignation, except in the case of dismissal, an employee will be paid at their wage rate on the date of resignation, for any remaining carryover PTO time and unused PTO time awarded in the current calendar year prorated by the number of months worked during that calendar year.

Example 1:

Employee A earns 203 hours of PTO on 1/1/19 and carried over 50 hours of PTO from 2018. They leave employment March 1, 2019 and used 25 PTO hours in January and February.

Employee A has worked for two twelfths of the calendar year. They are paid for 25 hours of PTO time carried over (50-25) plus one twelfth of 203 (16.92) for January and one twelfth of 203 (16.92) for February. The total hours paid out for is 25+16.92+16.92= 58.84

Example 2:

Employee B earns 32 hours of PTO on 1/1/19 and did not carry over any PTO hours from 2018. They leave employment July 1, 2019 and used 12 PTO hours from January thru June.

Employee B has worked for ½ of the calendar year. They are paid for a total of 4 hours upon termination. This is calculated by taking the 16 hours of PTO equal to working half of the calendar year and subtracting the 12 hours Employee B has used.

7.2 Sick Time

Under the Library's Paid-Time-Off model, employees no longer automatically accrue sick time hours, but may receive sick time hours based on their year-end PTO totals. If an employee maintains an existing balance, they may use their sick time hours balance in lieu of PTO for personal and immediate family illness (including pregnancy) or personal and immediate family medical appointments. Immediate family, for the purpose of sick time, is defined as children, spouse or domestic partner, parents, grandparents or other member of the household.

Figure 4.3. *(continued)*

A doctor's note is required for use of three or more consecutive days of sick time or when doubt exists about an employee's ability to work.

Sick time may be accrued up to 840 hours. Upon resignation, except in the case of dismissal, an employee with ten or more years of service will be paid at their wage rate on the date of resignation, for 10% of the unused sick time.

7.3 Time Off Without Pay
Employees may request Time Off Without Pay. Such requests must be approved by the employee's supervisor or the Director. The approval of requests may be affected by the scheduling needs of the Library.

7.4 Bereavement Leave
In the event of the death of an employee's spouse or domestic partner, parents and children (including foster and step), siblings, grandparents, grandchildren, mother-in-law, father-in-law, daughter-in-law, son-in-law, or other member of his/her household, benefit-eligible employees shall be excused from work at his/her request for a total not to exceed five working days, with pay. In the event of the death of the employee's uncle, aunt, cousin, brother-in-law, sister-in-law, or spouse or domestic partner's grandparents, the benefit-eligible employee shall be excused from work at his/her request for one day with pay.

7.5 Family and Medical Leave
As a public agency, the Library conforms to all requirements of the US Department of Labor Family and Medical Leave Act (FMLA), https://www.dol.gov/whd/fmla/. Below is summary information regarding family and medical leave benefits and eligibility.

In accordance with FMLA, the Library provides eligible employees:
- Up to 12 work weeks of unpaid leave a year,
- Maintains group health benefits during the leave as if employees continued to work instead of taking leave.
- Ensures the employee will return to their same or an equivalent job at the end of their FMLA leave.

Eligible employees may also take FMLA leave for specified reasons related to certain military deployments of their family members. Additionally, they may take up to 26 weeks of FMLA leave in a single 12-month period to care for a covered service member with a serious injury or illness.

When it is medically necessary, employees may take FMLA leave intermittently – taking leave in separate blocks of time for a single qualifying reason – or on a reduced leave schedule – reducing the employee's usual weekly or daily work schedule. Leave to care for or bond with a newborn child or for a newly placed adopted or foster child may only be taken intermittently with approval from the Library's Board of Trustees and must conclude within 12 months after the birth or placement.

Leave for the following events must be reported as family and medical leave:
- The birth of a child and the care of the newborn
- The placement of a child with an employee in connection with the adoption or state-approved foster care of the child
- The serious health condition of a child, parent, or spouse or domestic partner of the employee or a qualifying adult or child of a qualifying adult
- A serious health condition of the employee

- Qualifying exigencies arising out of the fact that the employee's spouse or domestic partner, son, daughter, or parent is on covered active duty or call to covered active duty status as a member of the National Guard, Reserves, or Regular Armed Forces

An eligible employee may elect to use all applicable accrued paid leave balances while taking family and medical leave. After an employee exhausts all paid leave or if the employee is requesting intermittent family and medical leave, the employee must submit a Family & Medical Leave Request to his or her immediate supervisor. For the period of the family and medical leave that is without pay, the employee on family and medical leave will continue to accrue service credit but will not accrue PTO and sick leave.

For the period of the family and medical leave that is without pay, the employee may continue health insurance benefits and will receive the premium sharing from the Library toward the cost of health insurance. The employee is responsible for self-paying by personal check or money order that part of his/her insurance cost that would otherwise be deducted from the employee's paycheck.

In order to be eligible to take leave under the FMLA, an employee must have worked 1,250 hours during the 12 months prior to the start of leave and have worked for the Library for 12 non-consecutive months within seven years of the leave request unless the break in service is due to an employee's fulfillment of military obligations.

Within five business days of the employee notifying the Library of their need for FMLA leave, the Library will provide the employee with a completed Notice of Eligibility and Rights & Responsiblities form and FMLA Designation Notice.

Leave covered under FMLA must be designated as FMLA-protected and the Library must inform the employee of the amount of leave that will be counted against the employee's FMLA leave entitlement. In order to determine whether leave is covered under the FMLA, the Library may request that the leave be supported by a certification. If the certification is incomplete or insufficient, the Library must state in writing what additional information is necessary to make the certification complete and sufficient. .

7.6 Cancer Screening Leave
New York State Civil Service Law entitles library employees to take up to four hours of paid leave annually, without charge to leave credits, for breast and prostate cancer screening. The screening includes physical exams, mammograms, and/or blood work specifically performed for the detection of breast or prostate cancer.

Cancer screening leave requests should be placed as off-site meeting requests. Travel time is included in the four -hour cap. Absence beyond the four hours must be charged to the employee's time off balances, or the time will be unpaid. The leave is not cumulative and expires at the close of business on the last day of each calendar year. Employees who undergo screenings outside of their regular work schedule do so on their own time.

To properly request this absence, the employee must receive prior approval by their supervisor. Satisfactory medical documentation, as determined by the director, is required after the employee's absence for this purpose.

7.6 Jury Duty
Employees should notify their supervisor or the Director upon receipt of a jury summons. Employees will be compensated for hours missed from work when they are required by a court to be present for jury duty. The employee should report to work during regularly scheduled hours when not occupied with court obligations.

Figure 4.3. *(continued)*

7.7 Voting Leave

The Library requests that, whenever possible, employees vote before or after work hours to avoid interference with business operations. However, if an employee does not have sufficient time outside of work hours to cast their ballot, the employee may be eligible for time off to vote. GPL may specify the hours during which the employee may take leave to vote. If there are fewer than four consecutive hours between the opening of the polls and the beginning of an employee's workday or between the end of an employee's workday and the closing of the polls, an employee may take up to three hours of paid leave to vote on Election Day. Employees must notify their employers of their need for time off to vote at least two working days before Election Day.

7.8 Military Leave

Employees who are enlisted in the military services, including the Ready Reserves and the National Guard, will be entitled to all rights and benefits afforded by federal and state law.

7.9 Crime Victims Leave

An employee may be entitled to leave to attend criminal justice proceedings if the employee, or their spouse or domestic partner, child, or parent, is a victim of a crime, is seeking an application or enforcement of a protection order, or is a witness in a criminal proceeding. Except in cases of imminent danger to the health or safety of the employee, or unless impracticable, an employee requesting crime victims leave must inform the Director prior to the date of their court appearance. Employees must be prepared to provide GPL with certification to verify the employee's eligibility for the leave requested, such as a police report, a court order, or evidence that they appeared in court.

Crime victims leave is unpaid; however, employees may use accrued PTO for this purpose.

7.10 Blood Donation Leave

Employees that work an average of 20 hours or more per week will be granted paid leave for blood donation that take place during a scheduled shift based on the table below:

Location of Blood Donation	Approved Frequency	Minimum Notice Required*
Onsite Red Cross blood drive	Two two-hour sessions per 12-month period	Two business days
Offsite location	Three hours of leave per 12-month period	Three business days

*If the donation leave time conflicts with an employee's scheduled desk or supervisory shift, they must provide at least one week's notice.

Employees must provide notice to either their supervisor or the Director. Offsite donations require the submission of an offsite meeting request via the Library's time management system.

7.11 Right of Nursing Mothers to Express Breast Milk

The Library shall provide reasonable unpaid break time, or permit an employee to use paid break time or meal time each day, to allow an employee to express breast milk for her nursing child for up to three years following childbirth. GPL shall make reasonable efforts to provide a room or other location, in close proximity to the work area, where an employee can express milk in privacy.

(continued)

GPL shall not discriminate in any way against an employee who chooses to express breast milk in the workplace.

7.12 Families First Coronavirus Response Act Leave
The Library will adhere to the provisions of The Families First Coronavirus Response Act (FFCRA). FFCRA requires certain employers to provide their employees with paid sick leave or expanded family and medical leave for specified reasons related to COVID-19.

In accordance with FFCRA and the Family and Medical Leave Act, the Library may require an employee to submit a certification from a health care provider to support the employee's need for FFCRA or FMLA leave to care for a covered family member with a serious health condition or for the employee's own serious health condition.

Information regarding FFCRA is available via this link, https://www.dol.gov/agencies/whd/pandemic.

7.12.1 Quarantine Leave
Quarantine leave is paid time off during a time of quarantine (which can be imposed, or self-imposed), as a specific policy allows.

If a full or part-time employee who is not personally ill is required to remain absent because of quarantine imposed by a governing authority, or if during a declared emergency an employee determines to self-quarantine and such employee presents a written statement of the attending physician or local health officer proving the necessity of such absence, such employee shall be granted leave with pay for the period of the required absence. Such pay shall cover the employee's routine hours (part-time hours will be based on an average of the most recent three pay periods, or as set by the board). Prior to return to duty, such employee may be required to submit a written statement, from the local health officer having jurisdiction, that return to duty will not jeopardize the health of other employees.

To be eligible for compensation during quarantine leave, employees must be ready, willing and able to work remotely on projects identified by library leadership during their regularly scheduled working hours, and must complete such duties as assigned. When performing tasks remotely, employees should note the time worked through the usual process for logging hours.

7.13 Additional New York State and Federal Leave Laws
The Library complies with all applicable New York State and Federal leave laws including those not expressly covered in this policy. Additional information regarding those leaves, as well as the leaves covered in this policy, is available via the NYS Department of Labor website.

8. Compensation Benefits

8.1 Social Security
As required by law, the Library pays the employer's portion of Social Security for each employee

8.2 Worker's Compensation
All employees are eligible for worker's compensation benefits for injuries sustained while working. Employees are required to immediately inform their supervisor or the Director of any injury occurring on the job and fill out an incident report and paperwork required by the state or the Library's insurance provider.

Figure 4.3. *(continued)*

8.3 Disability Benefits

All employees (except high school students working less than 35 hours a week) are covered by disability benefits insurance as required by law for non-work related disability. An employee may elect to use PTO and sick leave credits and the Library will request reimbursement provided by law when such credits are used for non-work related disability. The Library will credit the employee's sick bank for any reimbursement received from the disability insurance carrier.

8.4 New York State Retirement Participation

The Geneva Public Library is a participant in the New York State and Local Employees Retirement System, as of February 14, 2006. All employees (full time and part time) are eligible for the retirement system. Persons employed in temporary or part time positions may apply for membership but are not required to do so. Full-time employees hired after February 2006 are required to join the system as of the date of employment and will be covered by the provisions of the Retirement and Social Security Law.

The benefits determined by New York State Retirement System are based on the date of entry, tier, earnings, age and other matters.

8.5 Deferred Compensation Plans

All employees are eligible to enroll in the New York State Deferred Compensation Plan. Once enrolled, employees may set aside a portion of their wages, up to certain limits in accordance with State and Federal statutes. Participation in the plan is voluntary and the Library will work to provide training for employees interested in enrolling.

Effective May 25, 2016, employees may no longer purchase a tax sheltered annuity through MassMutual. However, employees who have previously purchased the Mass Mutual annuity may continue to defer a part of their present salary. Participation in the tax sheltered annuity program is voluntary.

8.6 Health and Dental Insurance

The Library provides staff who maintain a work schedule of 30 hours or more access to health and dental insurance for medical-care benefits. It determines the health insurance carrier and plans it makes available to staff. The plans, as well as summary information, are made available to staff during the Library's open enrollment period, which is held beginning in October each year. or at the start of employment for new hires.

Eligible staff may elect Single, Single and Spouse, Single and Child(ren), or Family coverage through an approved plan. Through payroll deduction, staff reimburse the Library for the difference between the Library's premium co-share benefit available to them and the cost of the additional coverage. Staff contributions towards health and dental insurance premiums are paid on a pre-tax basis without contribution limits.

Health and dental insurance elections must be made during the Library's open enrollment period or within two weeks following an applicable change of status event. Applicable change of status events include changes to: legal marital status, number of dependents, employment status, a dependent's eligibility status, and residence.

The Library's premium co-share benefit is set annually by the Board of Trustees. The co-share must meet the affordability and minimum value requirements determined by the IRS and the Affordable Care Act. For 2020, the co-share amount is $4,225 per year. The co-share is prorated based on the start date for new employees or the start/stop date of eligibility changes for current employees.

(continued)

The co-share must be first be applied to health insurance premiums. If the co-share is higher than the yearly cost of the health insurance premiums paid by an employee, the remaining amount of the co-share may only be applied to the employee's dental insurance premiums or to direct contributions to a health savings account (HSA) or flexible spending account (Health FSA) set up by the employee. Employees must complete a Remaining Health Insurance Co-share Election Form by the open enrollment period deadline or within two weeks of their official start date.

For the remaining co-share to be directed towards dental insurance premiums, an employee must also submit a dental plan enrollment application during the Library's open enrollment period, or within two weeks of your official start date if they are a new hire. For the remaining co-share to be directed towards an HSA or Health FSA, an employee must provide their HSA/Health FSA account information to the Library by the same deadline.

All staff with eligible health insurance plans purchased through the Library may elect to enroll in an HSA or Health FSA set up by the employee. Proof of enrollment, including relevant account information, must be submitted to the Finance Clerk or the Library Director in order to set up payroll deductions. Employees are responsible for ensuring the accuracy of the enrollment information, for complying with eligibility, contribution, and withdrawal rules, and for paying applicable fees to maintain the account. Contributions to HSA and Health FSA accounts will be made on a pre-tax basis.

Contributions to HSA and Health FSA accounts will be made on a pre-tax basis. For 2020, the contribution limits are the following:
- HSA Accounts: $3,550 for an individual and $7,100 for a family
- Health FSA Accounts: $2,750

Staff that maintain a work schedule of 30 hours or more per week, who decline coverage and receive health insurance coverage from an eligible source other than the library, shall receive an annual stipend, paid in June, in the amount of 10% of the amount of the Library's yearly health care premium co-share benefit. If coverage is obtained from another source for a partial period, the stipend will be prorated based on the amount of time in the previous fiscal year the employee did not purchase coverage through the Library. To decline coverage, staff must complete a Waiver of Group Coverage form must completed by the open enrollment period deadline or within two weeks on an employee's start date for new hires.

A change in employment classification that would result in loss of eligibility to participate in an approved health insurance plan qualifies an employee for benefits continuation under the Consolidated Omnibus Budget Reconciliation Act (COBRA).

9. Benefits Upon Leaving
Upon leaving library employment, all employee benefits will be discontinued, with the exception of any continuation required by Federal or New York State employment laws. Employees will be paid for accrued PTO time, and if eligible, for 10% of accrued sick time, as described in the sections above.

10. Outside Services and Consulting for Professional Staff
The Library is supportive of its staff providing outside services to the public for compensation that is separate from the compensation they receive as an employee of the Library, and for services that are similar to those the staff is responsible for providing to the public as an employee of the library, with the following provisions:

Figure 4.3.   *(continued)*

- There are no deficiencies in the staff's job performance as a result of providing these outside services.
- The planning and delivery of these outside services are to be done on the staff's own time, taking PTO time as necessary.
- Recipients of these outside services are informed that the services are not provided by the Geneva Public Library and that the Library in no way takes responsibility for these services.
- The Library must be compensated for the use of office supplies and equipment in preparing and conducting these outside services, and compensated for the use of materials and services for which the public is charged to access or use.
- There is no conflict of interest by the staff when developing his or her outside services and developing similar services as an employee of the Library and provided to the public.

11. Internal Communication

Effective and ongoing communication within the Library is essential. As such, GPL maintains systems through which important information can be shared by employees and management.

Bulletin boards are posted in designated areas of the workplace to display important information and announcements regarding library trainings. In addition, the Library uses email and an online communication document, available on all staff computers, to facilitate communication and share access to documents. In instances where staff do not have access to or the expectation of checking email or the online document, or in instances where privacy or regulation stipulates, employees will be informed of library news via confidential letters or in-person communication.

All employees are responsible for checking internal communications on a frequent and regular basis. Employees are also responsible for attending the Library's Staff Development Days and other Communication Meetings to the best of their ability given the limitations of their work schedules and other commitments. Employees should consult their supervisor with any questions or concerns on information disseminated.

12. Facility Access

All regular full-time and part-time GPL employees, with the exception of Library Pages, will be issued a key and security code to gain access to the building. Library Clerk Subs will be issued security codes upon the start of employment and may be issued keys at the discretion of the Director.

All lost or stolen keys must be reported to the Director as soon as possible. Upon separation from GPL, and at any other time upon the Library's request, all keys must be returned to the Director.

13. Performance Evaluation

All staff shall receive, at least once a year, a performance review that objectively assesses their performance and accomplishments relative to the job description and annual goals. All staff shall also receive a Professional Development Plan that includes the specific tasks and goals for their position for the next year by which the staff member shall be evaluated.

The Director shall be evaluated by the Board of Trustees. The Director shall determine the evaluation procedure for all other employees.

14. Discipline/Termination

The Library follows the disciplinary and termination procedures established by New York State Civil Service Law when addressing staff incompetence or misconduct. General guidelines related to removal

(continued)

and disciplinary action for NYS Civil Service employees are available here,
http://www.nysl.nysed.gov/libdev/excerpts/cvs75.htm

15. Resignation

All professional positions (Library Director, Librarians, Library Assistants, and Finance Clerk) are to give at least one month's written notice at the time of resignation. All others are to give two weeks written notice. Failure to give such notice may result in loss of accrued benefits.

16. Changes

These policies are subject to change at the discretion of the Board of Trustees.

Adopted by the Board of Trustees: March 9, 2006
Amended by the Board of Trustees: 7/26/2007, 5/28/2008, 7/30/2008, 5/27/2009, 4/28/2010, 5/26/2010, 9/27/2010, 10/30/2013, 7/30/2014, 11/19/2014, 10/28/15, 2/17/2016, 5/25/2016, 7/27/2016, 1/25/2017, 4/26/2017, 5/31/2017, 8/30/2017, 12/20/2017, 1/31/2018, 4/25/2018, 10/24/2018, 1/30/2019, 3/27/2019, 4/29/2019, 10/30/2019, 01/29/2020, 5/29/2020

Figure 4.3. *(continued)*

Bibliography

Hall, Kate, and Kathy Parker. 2019. *The Public Library Director's Toolkit*. Chicago: American Library Association.

Prentice, Ann E. 2011. *Public Libraries in the 21st Century*. Santa Barbara, CA: Libraries Unlimited.

Reid, Ian. 2017. "The 2017 Public Library Data Service Report: Characteristics and Trends." *Public Libraries* 56, no. 5 (September/October): 20–30. http://publiclibrariesonline.org.

CHAPTER 5

ADVOCACY AND RELATIONSHIPS WITH EXTERNAL GROUPS AND STATE AND LOCAL GOVERNMENT

- Advocacy
- Local government
- State government
- Federal government
- Friends of the Library
- Library foundations
- Friends and foundation merged
- Local organizations and groups
- State library associations

Advocacy

Advocacy is defined as "planned, deliberate, sustained effort to develop understanding and support incrementally over time" (Stenstrom and Haycock 2015). Public librarians can advocate to patrons, government officials, stakeholders, policy makers, and business and community leaders. Advocacy requires working to create an understanding of the value of public libraries that should help those making funding decisions to make favorable decisions about the library's budget. Recent studies have indicated that many people do not know what the library does or what its funding sources are. As a result it is important to improve public awareness of libraries and what they do.

Many librarians and library staff confuse advocacy and lobbying. Advocacy is about educating policy makers on specific issues. Library staff, the board of trustees, members of the Friends of the Library, and library users can advocate for the library. Anyone can advocate for a specific issue, but lobbying is about influencing a particular vote. Yet for many, lobbying must be done outside the workplace because it will not be legal for them to lobby on work time. Lobbying often involves going with a library affiliated group to an event where the group comes with the aim of trying to get particular legislative bills passed. It could be at the local, state, or federal level. Library associations often organize a day of lobbying and train librarians how to do this effectively. This includes visiting the offices of their elected officials.

Advocacy is part of a librarian's job. It is not something that happens once a year when there is a vote on the budget. Rather, it is something that is constantly being worked on throughout the year. The library director, the staff, the trustees, and other library supporters must work to build positive, personal relationships with those who make decisions about the library's budget. This may mean meeting formally with the decision makers as well as informally by attending local council meetings or by attending local events and having a chance to get to know the decision makers on a more personal basis. Listening is very important. Finding out the interests of the legislators and what their goals are for the community is important so that the library can decide how it fits with these goals. Relationship building is at the heart of advocacy. It will mean providing information on library activities on an ongoing basis throughout the year and stories about library successes. Just providing data is not enough. It's the library stories about how patrons have used the library to achieve their goals that the legislators and their staffs will remember. The library must also provide good customer service at all times. All of this will help develop the credibility of the library so that decision makers will have a favorable impression of the library when budget decisions are being made. If nothing has been done during the year, external pressure at the end of the budget process will probably not bring the results the library wants and needs.

Studies about working with decision makers provide some insight for librarians on how to impact their decision makers. Decision makers are influenced by people with authority or expertise whom they respect; these individuals might be members of the board of trustees, members of the Friends of the Library, or other influential people who use or support the library. Decision makers like consistency, so it is important that they understand the library's values and beliefs as well as the library's future plans as stated in the library's strategic plan. These decision makers need to like a group in order to want to support it, making it important to be in continual contact with those in positions of power. They believe in reciprocity, so if the library has invited them to visit and has made it newsworthy, then the decision maker will owe the library. They will also follow the lead of their peers from other municipalities, so if their peers think well of their library, they probably will too (Stenstrom and Haycock 2015).

Advocacy includes the following:

- Promotion. The library can develop a library brand, use the library's website effectively to promote services and events, and use social media to connect with their users.

- Public relations. The library can send out press releases and news items to provide information about its programs and services.

- Marketing. The library can participate in or develop surveys to find out more about its community and target certain groups in their community for special promotion.

- Networking. The library can reach out to local groups and organizations to promote the library's programs and services and to find out what other groups and organizations have to offer. This can provide opportunities to create partnerships.

- Persuasion. This involves calling for collaboration with other groups. (Stenstrom 2018)

Here are some concrete ways that libraries can perform advocacy:

- Use well-known community people to advocate for the library by talking about its successes. These advocates might be members of the board of trustees, members of the Friends of the Library, people who use the library on a regular basis, or members of other community groups who work with the library.

- Train the library staff to provide information about the library to its users and to provide positive customer service throughout the year, to treat users with courtesy and respect, and to be approachable. Be ready to assist local government officials with needed information.

- Encourage the members of the board of trustees to use their community connections on behalf of the library, to get to know key government officials, to attend local council meetings, to be ready to respond to questions about the library, and to join and work with the statewide library trustees organization.

- Encourage the Friends of the Library to build public awareness and support for the library, form partnerships with local community groups, and engage in word-of-mouth marketing.

- Provide information about the library through its newsletter, its website, social media sites, general promotional materials, letters to the editor, op-ed pieces, radio and TV, and presentations in the community.

- Get to know elected officials, legislators, and their staffs. Listen to what they say are local needs. Invite elected officials and legislators to library events so they can see what the library does, and arrange a photo op to make the visit newsworthy. Photo ops with children are always good, such as handing out certificates at the end of the summer reading club.

- Thank public officials for their support publicly.

Case Study 1

A public library director from a small public library offered this advice about working with local government. She said it is important to work with many government departments who can then talk about the library. The director does an American Library Association (ALA)–type Read poster each year, featuring someone in the local government with a favorite book they have chosen. It is hung in the library, but they also get a copy for their office. The library staff also does regular programming featuring government workers and departments, such as inviting the fire department to bring their fire truck during a children's program or "Coffee with a Cop" so people can come to meet a police person, ask questions, and talk with them. All this helps the library at budget time since there are more government people to lend their name to support for the library's budget.

Case Study 2

Another library director reported that the library was told on a Monday that the county planned to cut their funding in half. The library sent very targeted emails (only about 350 were sent), wrote a Facebook post, and rallied trustees and foundation members to attend the Wednesday county budget work session. By the afternoon the cut was off the table. The community stepped up in a big way. This demonstrates how long-term advocacy works. This library did not suddenly have an emergency funding need and have to start from scratch. They had been building relationships all along so that a plan was already in place to deal with a budget cut.

Case Study 3

A large city library system trained its entire staff to do advocacy work. Some staff members just talked to library users, some talked to friends and neighbors about the library, and some went to community board meetings to report on what the library was doing. It is valuable to train all the staff so the word about the library will permeate the entire community.

Advocacy is not a onetime thing. In order to influence local officials of the need for library funding, librarians and the board of trustees must have worked consistently during the year. They need to convince those with authority to make decisions that the library values are the same as theirs. The people speaking for the library will have earned their respect, and during the year they will have gotten to know the library director and some members of the board of trustees and liked what they saw (Stenstrom 2018). Many libraries do a ROI (return on investment) chart that shows how much the library contributes to the community. See an ROI example (value calculator) in chapter 6.

Local Government

Many public libraries are part of the local government and are dependent on the local government for their budget. This requires understanding how the local government works and providing information throughout the year on the public library. If the library is a department of local government or funded almost completely by local government, then the board of trustees will be advisory concerning the budget. But the board of trustees will still be responsible for policy-making. The library will want to develop a close working relationship with local government. It will want to use the services of local government when available and get to know the department heads and other officials in the government. By developing these relationships it will strengthen the role of the library and provide another level of advocacy. The public library director may attend regular meetings of the local government and have a chance to talk about the library even briefly. Working cooperatively with the local government units is a good way to spread the word about the library. This could be done in a variety of ways, but programming is one of them. The library could feature speakers from various units of the local government as part of their programming or feature programs on topics of current interest to the community. Tours of the library or participation at programs by government officials is also useful, giving them an opportunity for photos and press coverage.

State Government

For many public libraries there are not strong connections with state government. This is mostly because only small amounts of money come from the state. At the state government level there is usually an office of library services that is mainly for public libraries but may support other kinds of libraries too. Often there is state legislation that provides funding for public libraries. The way this legislation is written varies greatly from state to state. Sometimes funds can go directly to public libraries as state aid or grants, and other times it is for services to the libraries developed by the state library, such as online databases available to all or grants for which the libraries can apply. If funding goes to the public libraries in the form of state aid, the libraries will probably have to meet some minimum qualifications that will vary from state to state. The funding is usually administered by the office of library services. It is important that public libraries and their trustees are familiar with the services of the state library and the library development office. State library associations often organize a lobbying day to promote state legislation, and public libraries should participate in this event. Even though the amount of state funding for an individual library may be small, this funding is needed and can make a big difference for some libraries. During the year the library should stay in touch with their elected officials in the state government so they are aware of the programs and services of their library. Invitations to events and tours will keep them knowledgeable about the work the library is doing in the community.

Federal Government

Federal library legislation provides funding to state government that trickles down in the form of grants or state services to libraries. Sometimes it is hard to see the direct benefit of this funding, but it is of vital importance to libraries nationwide. The American Library Association has an office in Washington, D.C., the Public Policy and Advocacy office, that monitors library and other related legislation. Once a year librarians go to Washington, D.C., to lobby for library legislation and talk to their representatives in the House of Representatives and their senators in the Senate about libraries and the need for this legislation. Sometimes there is other federal legislation with grants for which libraries can apply.

Friends of the Library

Friends of the Library is an important group for the library. Friends can use local energy in an organized way and turn support into action. With appropriate guidance, the Friends of the Library can make significant contributions. Friends can

- raise money for the library,

- provide volunteers to work in the library,

- promote the library in the community,

- provide program and collection support, and

- advocate for the library.

Friends are usually established as a 501(c)(3) so that they are nonprofit and tax exempt. In order to apply for a 501(c)(3), the Friends group must have bylaws and an organizational structure such as officers and committees. Many Friends of the Library groups run book sales or raise money through specific annual fundraising events such as author luncheons. This money is then given to the library often for specific purposes, such as collections and programs. But the Friends can also be useful for raising capital money for a new library building or a library renovation. A well-organized Friends group can be tremendously helpful to the library both as a fundraising arm and as a way to carry the library message into the community.

Friends groups require direction from the library director so it is clear how they can be most useful. The Friends group will want to develop close relationships with the library director and the board of trustees and to appoint a liaison to each one. It is recommended that the Friends write up an operating agreement with the library explaining how the money they raise will be spent, what support they can expect from the library, and who will approve, for example, an advocacy campaign. The operating agreement could include

- fundraising priorities,

- how the money raised will be spent,

- a specific time for an annual meeting to discuss plans for the year,

- what other kinds of library support the Friends will provide,

- who will approve the advocacy plan, and

- what the Friends' role in programming will be.

Even though the board of trustees and the Friends work together, they should be completely separate. Members of the board of trustees can join the Friends but should not serve as officers. In addition to volunteer activities such as fundraising projects, members of the Friends often work in the library on a volunteer basis. The Friends officers should meet frequently with the library director to find out how they can support the library through fundraising or through other activities. Once they raise funds they will want to discuss with the library director how the funds will be used.

Table 5.1. Comparison of Friends of the Library and board of trustees roles

Role of Friends of the Library	Role of Board of Trustees
Support library policies	Review and approve library policies
Fundraise for the library	Participate in fundraising for the library
Support the library budget	Review and approve the library budget
Provide volunteers for the library	Approve paid library positions
Advocate for the library	Advocate for the library
Assist with long-range planning	Take a leadership role in long-range planning

If the director wants to establish a Friends group, here are some steps to consider:

1. Find a core group of users who want to form a Friends group.

2. Develop an operating agreement with the library.

3. Develop a structure for the Friends group.

4. Write bylaws and apply for a 501(c)(3).

5. Develop a dues structure.

6. Develop a member recruitment campaign.

Friends groups should always be planning ahead. There should be an effort to continue to recruit new members to sustain the energy of the group. There should also be a plan for some rotation of officers. Fresh ideas are always needed, so it is important to have new members of the leadership group.

Case Study

The Friends of the St. Paul (Minnesota) Public Library are a vibrant Friends group and a most interesting group. They have their own website—thefriends.org—and even their own strategic plan. This Friends group began in 1945, so it has a very long history. Its mission is to "act as a catalyst for libraries to strengthen and inspire their communities." They raise funds to support the St. Paul Public Library, including money for many literary programs, and advocate for the library throughout the year. In addition to supporting the work of the St. Paul Public Library, this Friends group provides assistance to other Friends group nationwide through a consulting service.

Library Foundations

Many public libraries have set up foundations. Foundations are more formal and are a way for people to donate larger sums of money, stocks, real estate, and so forth to the library, and with 501(c)(3) status the donations are tax deductible. Foundations meet the need for funding large projects and meeting long-term goals. Foundations are useful because they can work in ways that the library cannot work when funded by government funds since they have private funds.

Foundations are set up following guidelines for foundations. They must have a lawyer prepare Articles of Incorporation and apply for 501(c)(3) status so that donors will have a tax deduction for gifts. Foundations will have a separate board of directors and officers. The structure can vary depending on how it is organized. The foundation can establish its own rules and can invest the funds donated until they are needed.

Funds raised by the foundation will be for projects beyond the public funding that is for the annual operation of the library. Larger donations are possible through planned giving and bequests. The donors (individuals or businesses or foundations) can be assured that their donations will go for a specific project. Many libraries use the funds from the foundation as part of the funding for a new building, an addition to the building, or additional programming or collections. Foundations are also eligible for some grants.

Although many foundations are relatively new, the Seattle Public Library Foundation (supportspl.org) was formed in the 1980s. Their website provides a great deal of information about this foundation. An annual report gives the user a good idea of what the foundation does. There is information on how to contribute both as an individual and as a business or foundation. The foundation has funded mobile library service, museum passes, author programs, and writing classes.

The Rochester (Minnesota) Library Foundation has as its mission "to raise private funds for educational and informational resources and projects in a manner that does not diminish the need for strong public funding, and to educate the community about the Library's vital role in meeting our community's need." This foundation provides annual reports and has the support of many businesses and institutions in the community. The foundation has funded a Wi-Fi hotspot program, a literacy program, and pilot programming on diversity and inclusion.

Friends and Foundation Merged

Some libraries are now choosing to have a merged Friends group and foundation. The Friends of the St. Paul Public Library is an example of such a merger. Those libraries who have chosen a merged organization find that it is less confusing for the public. Users don't have to decide which group to contact for a donation; rather, the group members themselves will decide. Many don't even use the word *foundation* in their name but are simply a Friends group that also handles the work of a foundation. It is also less administrative work for the groups involved and for the library administration.

Local Organizations and Groups

Local organizations and groups can lend support to the library, and the library in turn can partner with them for programming or other events. If the library has partners, they can help to publicize the program, adding to the number of people who participate in the program. The more that the public library works with local groups, the stronger the library's visibility will be in the community. Some public libraries have sent staff members to particular groups to see how they could be of service to them. They might find that the group is planning a project that will benefit from library research. For example, the chamber of commerce wants to assist local business in economic development. The library might do some research on new ideas for small business development. In that case the staff member assigned to the group will undertake this research. Such a project is an attempt to show local groups how the library can assist them and make their work easier.

State Library Associations

State library associations can be quite useful at the state and local levels. First of all, they offer a way for the staff to learn new ideas and new strategies. There are two levels of state library associations. One level is the continuing education they offer that often includes an annual conference or sometimes regional meetings during the year. The second level is the work done to promote library development through contact with state government officials and state government representatives. Often state library associations offer workshops on advocacy work that can add to the local library's knowledge. State library associations are a valuable group for all public libraries.

In conclusion, advocacy is an essential ingredient for all public libraries. It is not enough just to run a good public library and to promote the library annually to get a budget passed. Good advocacy is a year-round program. The public library should involve as many people as possible in advocacy work. Everyone should be continually aware of the public library and what contribution it is making to the local community.

All levels of government contribute to successful public libraries. Libraries must be aware of what their role should be with each level. Concentration is often on the local level, but libraries should be aware of the contributions of state and federal government and participate in efforts to gain funding for public libraries at these levels too.

Friends of the Library and library foundations provide another level of support for public libraries. They are a way of gaining monetary support, volunteers, and knowledge of the work of the library throughout the community.

Discussion Questions

1. What could a small library do to develop an advocacy program?

2. Are you aware of how your local public library gets its funding?

Bibliography

Stenstrom, Cheryl. 2018. "Advocacy." In *Information Services Today: An Introduction*, 2nd ed., edited by Sandra Hirsh (343–54). Lanham, MD: Rowman & Littlefield.

Stenstrom, Cheryl, and Ken Haycock. 2015. "Public Library Advocacy: An Evidence-Based Perspective on Sustainable Funding." *Public Libraries* 54, no. 4 (July/August): 38–41.

United for Libraries. 2012. "Libraries Need Friends: A Toolkit to Create Friends Groups or to Revitalize the One You Have." www.ala.org/united/friends.

United for Libraries. 2017. "United for Libraries Resources." www.ala.org/united/foundations.

CHAPTER 6

FISCAL ORGANIZATION OF PUBLIC LIBRARIES
Funding, Funding Sources, and Budgets

- Strategic planning and the budget
- Funding sources
- Local funds
- State funds
- Federal funds
- Gifts and donations
- Fundraising
- Endowments and bequests
- Grants
- Types of budgets
- Budget years
- Preparing the budget
- Budget approval cycle and budget presentation
- Financial control and budget management
- Dealing with budget cuts
- Value of library service

E ven though libraries are considered a public good, funding public libraries has always been challenging. There are many demands on most municipal budgets for funding, such as the police department and the fire department, so that libraries often fall to the bottom of the list or are at least not near the top. Efforts are needed on a year-round basis to keep the library's programs, services, and needs before the funding bodies. Advocacy by many who support the public library is needed to make it possible to maintain and increase funding. The more visible the library is in the community, the better chance it will have to receive the operating funds it needs. In this chapter the emphasis will be on planning and presenting the library budget so that the funding agency will understand why the library funding is needed.

Strategic Planning and the Budget

The library budget should reflect both the library's short- and long-range strategic plans. It is a contract with the community and provides information as to what the library plans to accomplish. The library's plan should show that future needs and directions have been carefully thought out. Therefore, there should not be many surprises in the budget. It is assumed that the governing body to which the library reports will have seen the strategic plan and agreed on its general direction. The plan will reflect observed and projected changes in the community and possible new partnerships that make new programs and services possible. Sometimes changes are faster than predicted, such as sudden population changes that will be explained when the budget is presented to the governing body and to the community.

Funding Sources

A public library is usually supported by local funds from tax sources. If a public library is supported by local government funds, then it is subject to the laws and regulations that govern the source of the library's primary income. Public libraries may receive funds not only from local government sources but also from the state and federal government as well as gifts, fundraising, endowments, and grants. A footnote to this is that there are a small number of public libraries completely supported by private funds or primarily by private funds.

Local Funds

Local funds can come from a variety of sources. If the library is part of the local government, funds may come from the general funds of the municipal-

Table 6.1.   Public library funding sources

Local funds (municipalities, townships, counties, etc.)	This is a major source of funding for most public libraries.
State funds	Many states provide individual libraries or public library systems with some funding.
Federal funds	Most federal funds are allocated to states; the funds in turn can be allocated to local libraries.
Gifts and donations	Many libraries receive gifts and donations from their grateful users.
Endowments and bequests	Libraries with foundations seek out endowments and bequests.
Grants	Libraries often apply for and receive grants for new projects.
Fundraising	Libraries and their Friends groups often raise funds from fundraising events such as book sales and special events.
Miscellaneous income	Fines and fees are often collected by the library, though many public libraries are no longer collecting fines.

ity, county, township, and so forth. A major source of local funds is property taxes. In this case the library may be asked to attend a local government meeting and make a presentation about its budget needs for the coming year. Then the governing body allocates funds to the library based on the library's budget proposal and available funds. Finally, the library may be designated to receive a percentage of some fees or taxes that the municipality collects. Other funding discussed in this chapter should be considered supplemental funding. The major funding source should not cut the library's budget just because the library receives additional funding from other sources. This is an important concept to establish.

In other cases there might be a library tax that is voted on separately by the local citizens; this tax is usually based on real estate or property taxes or perhaps sales tax. The library will then receive funding based on a positive vote. In this case the library may not be as closely related to the local government and may not be bound by their rules.

State Funds

Many states have successfully passed legislation that provides funding to public libraries. This might be actual funds granted to each public library if they meet certain criteria, such as the number of hours open, the necessary number of professional librarians, or local funding requirements, or it could be funding to library systems that will in turn provide services to the libraries in the system. Sometimes additional funding is available for rural libraries. In New Jersey, for example, a municipality is eligible for state funding aid based on the local per capita aid provided to the library or libraries. In Pennsylvania, in order to be eligible to receive state aid, the local financial effort of a library or library system must be at least $5 per capita unless the library serves an economically distressed municipality. Or the state funds might go to library systems to be used on behalf of all the libraries in the system.

State library agencies also offer many services to public libraries at no charge, such as continuing education seminars, reference services, consulting services, and assistance with grants.

Federal Funds

Federal funds for libraries usually come from the IMLS (Institute of Museum and Library Services; https://imls.gov). The IMLS awards funds to each state from the Library Services and Technology Act (LSTA), and each state can distribute these funds. Often the state library will develop programs to use the federal money, such as paying for online databases for the state as a whole or for interlibrary loan. Other IMLS funds are awarded through grants for collection preservation, Native American library services, community catalyst grants, and grants for small and rural libraries. Libraries can apply for these grants individually. Sometimes other grant programs at the federal level list public libraries as a group eligible to apply. These can be found through the website www.grants.gov. The ALA's Public Policy and Advocacy office (www.ala.org/aboutala/offices/WO) is also a good source for finding out about these grants.

Gifts and Donations

Libraries often receive monetary gifts for some specific purpose, such as in honor or memory of someone. The monetary gifts are often for the collection so the library will be able to purchase additional materials. But donations could also be for capital projects—a new building, a renovation, or new furniture. Gifts can come from individuals or from organizations such as the Friends of the Library or the local Kiwanis club. Library foundations are useful in attracting large donations.

Fundraising

The library itself may undertake fundraising to bolster the library's budget through events or by contacting people, organizations, or businesses in the community and asking for donations, or the Friends of the Library may organize a fundraising event in order to provide additional funds to the library. The fundraising can take the form of an event such as a dinner or a luncheon with an author speaking or can be a book sale. The funds received might be used for collections, programs, or other needs the director has identified.

Endowments and Bequests

Many libraries are now setting up foundations for planned giving in the form of endowments and bequests to encourage more people to give larger monetary gifts to the library. In addition to monetary gifts, the foundation usually accepts stocks, real estate, and so forth. These foundations are set up as a 501(c)(3) in order to make it possible for individuals who contribute to receive a tax deduction. The structure of the foundation can vary, but it will usually have a separate board of trustees and officers, and will usually be separate from the Friends group. Foundation money is separate from the library's annual budget. Funds given to the foundation can be spent over a period of time and usually not all in one year.

Grants

Libraries often apply for grants from the state or federal government or from private funders such as foundations that provide grants to gain additional funds. Grants are useful to fund a new project not yet tested, such as a cooperative project with the schools, a program for immigrants, or an expansion of children's services. If the project is successful, the library may be able to justify requesting local funding to continue it. A good way to find appropriate grants is through the Foundation Directory Online (FDO) Professional, which lists foundations and businesses that regularly provide grants. The directory can be searched by type of organization funded, such as libraries, and in what states the foundation or business supplies funds and the range of monetary funding usually provided to a specific organization or project.

Types of Budgets

The budget documents the programs and services of the library as well as defines the level of particular services by the funds requested. The budget shows the library's plan in numbers for the year and refers indirectly to its short- and long-term goals. Libraries have an operating budget, which is developed annually for the fiscal year, and a capital budget, which is for major expenditures above a certain dollar amount for such projects as a remodeling or construction program or technology—perhaps an upgrade to an ILS—that can extend over several years. Most annual operating budgets are either a line-item budget or a program budget.

Line-Item Budgets

Line-item budgets are the most common type of operating budgets found in public libraries. It lists each revenue category—such as local, state, and federal funds; grants; and fines and fees—and each expenditure category, such as personnel costs (salaries and fringe benefits), materials for the collection, electricity, telephone, insurance, equipment, supplies, and postage. It is an easy budget to develop and an easy one to understand. It is also useful because it follows a template and can be compared to previous-year budgets. The problem with a line-item budget is that it does not show how the parts of the budget are connected. For that reason it is an easy budget to cut. But a percentage cut in the budget or the elimination of a line in the budget may produce unintended consequences, such as not having enough funding for the children's summer reading program.

Here is an example of a line-item budget:

Table 6.2. Example of line-item budget

Revenue	Comments
Local funding	Funding from the local government or from local taxes
State funding	Grants to individual libraries through state allocations
Federal funding	LSTA funds distributed through the state or other federal funding
Grants	Grants applied for and received by the library
Fines and fees	Income collected by the library for fines, copying fees, meeting room rentals, etc.

Expenditures	
Salaries	The total cost of all salaries for both full-time and part-time staff
Fringe benefits	Includes health insurance, social security, retirement plans, workers' compensation, unemployment, etc.
Materials	Includes all kinds of library materials—books, magazines, audiovisual, e-books, databases—both purchased and leased

Expenditures	Comments
Programming	Includes fees for speakers and performers, supplies for programs, etc.
Equipment and furniture	Includes equipment needed, such as new chairs and tables, and shelving
Supplies	Includes office supplies, custodial supplies, etc.
Technology	Includes computers, printers, computer supplies, etc.
Contractual services	Includes contracts for ILS services, payroll, legal services, audits, etc.
Utilities	Includes heating, lighting, telephone, water, etc.
Insurance	Includes building insurance and related on-the-job insurance
Travel	Includes local travel, conference travel, etc.
Training	Includes registration fees for conferences and for sending staff to training outside the library
Marketing	Includes ads, newsletters, postage, etc.

See a sample line-item budget at the end of the chapter.

Program Budgets

A Program budget organizes a budget by each program in the library and is useful in that it shows the cost of each program. The program budget shows better how things fit together and shows the cost of an individual program or service. If cuts are made, it is easier to protect a program or cut a percentage of a program. Some examples of programs are circulation services, reference services, children's services, adult services, technology services, maintenance services, and administration overhead.

Here is an example of a program budget for reference services:

Table 6.3. Example of program budget for reference services

Expenditures	Comments
Salaries for reference staff	Includes full-time and part-time staff
Fringe benefits for reference staff	Cost of social security, health insurance, retirement plans, etc.
Materials	Includes print and electronic reference resources— purchases and leases
Staff training	Includes registration and travel for staff
Indirect costs	Includes a percentage of administrative costs, marketing costs, and technology costs

This program budget for reference services can be backed up with statistics about the use of reference services and some qualitative information as well, such as comments from users of the service.

Line-item budgets and program budgets both have their pros and cons. Line-item budgets are easy to compile, and they can be compared from one year to the next. Changes in particular lines can easily be explained. For example, more funds might now be going into e-resources and less into print resources. But line-item budgets are the easiest for a funder to cut. They can just pick out lines that are not fixed amounts and cut them.

Program budgets on the other hand show what is needed to run a particular program, so it is harder to cut one element in it without damaging the program. It is also useful in the library to see how much particular programs cost.

Capital Budgets

In addition to the annual operating budget, libraries often have a capital budget. This budget is dedicated to larger projects and purchases, and may be a multiyear budget. A capital budget may be for a new library, an addition to the existing library, or a new integrated library system. The library may need more than one source of funding to accomplish the project, so some money may be local money, some from the state, and some from the library's foundation and grant funding.

Budget Years

Budget years are usually January 1 to December 31 or July 1 to June 30. This usually depends on the major source of local funds. The library may have to deal with other budget years as well if it receives funds from other sources that require reporting at the end of their fiscal year. The state budget is often on a different budget year, or a federal grant could also have a different budget year. So the library must be prepared to make reports to others who have different budget years.

Preparing the Budget

Preparing the budget begins several months before it is due. In fact, some information for the next budget is collected year round. If there is a budget office, even if it is only one person, it is updating the information on the community, including demographic information, looking at internal and external changes, and monitoring changes in the law or in prices. For example, a change in the minimum wage or in fringe benefits, or a change in prices, such as an increase in the cost of paper or in e-products, will certainly affect the library.

Preparing the budget involves first examining last year's budget to see if the estimates as to how much was needed in each category were accurate. It may be that things have changed so that some estimates were too high and others too low. Maybe the library is subscribing to more electronic resources and buying fewer print books or fewer periodicals. It is important to examine this and change the estimates for the next year based on the more recent projections. Often it is useful to go back to vendors to check the numbers and make sure that the best price estimates are still valid. For materials, vendors that are used are often helpful in providing estimates for the next year. For example, the vendor for periodicals and serials will be able to tell you if you need to increase the estimate for the periodicals and serials the library is acquiring. Another way to get costs of library materials is from annual articles in *Library Journal* and *Publishers Weekly* with estimates of prices for the next year. Department heads should also be involved in the development of the budget. They can provide more detailed information on both what is needed for the next year and information about why their budget lines were either over or under the estimated amounts.

The largest part of a budget is personnel costs, which include salaries and fringe benefits such as social security, health insurance, and retirement benefits. It is important to follow information about these benefits so that the library is aware of any changes. The library may have a salary scale that it follows for the staff based on years of service, or it may decide on an increase in salaries based on a percentage of the present salaries that will be given for the following year. The library may also have a library union contract with a salary schedule to be followed. Salaries, fringe benefits, and such costs as electricity, telephone, and heating/cooling are often called fixed costs since they are set and are nonnegotiable. Other costs are variable costs, such as collection and program costs.

The library will continue to build the next year's budget throughout the year. Data gathering is extremely important, as is knowledge of changes in the community that might affect the library. Data gathering might include circulation statistics, attendance at library programs, reference statistics, and costs of materials purchased for the collection. In presenting the funding needed for the next year, a department head should refer to information derived from internal and external data. This will provide a more solid justification.

Table 6.4.   Data sources

Local surveys	This could be local government or a local organization; local surveys are very useful.
Federal census data	The census numbers are now updated frequently so changing demographics can be identified.
Circulation statistics	Circulation can produce statistics by age, languages spoken, etc., depending on what users provide when they register for a library card.
Program attendance statistics	The number of people attending each program and whatever additional information is collected.
Reference statistics	The number of people requesting assistance with information needs.
Materials purchased or leased for the library	The number of materials purchased or leased, the average cost and the subject, the format and intended user group, such as children.
Outreach statistics	This can include all sorts of library outreach to groups and organizations.
External sources	Information about the community gained from local government and local organizations.

Budget Approval Cycle and Budget Presentation

The library should have a finance committee to participate in developing the budget. The members of the committee will vary but might include the library's budget officer, the library director, a representative of the board of trustees, a staff representative, and perhaps a representative from the Friends of the Library. Once the director and finance committee have completed the budget, it is presented to the board of trustees, and the board members then review it, ask questions, and make suggestions for changes. After the board of trustees' approval, there may be more layers of approval, which could include a review or hearing by a local government committee and a final approval by the governing body of the local government. In other cases the budget may be separate from the local government's budget and the local residents vote directly on the budget.

The budget presentation may start with the board of trustees, but then the library will usually have to give a presentation to the governing body or to the community depending on how the budget is approved. The library director and the board of trustees should be well prepared for this presentation with appropriate data to explain the budget. It is usually good to have some graphs or charts to show trends or comparisons. For example, with a line-item budget there could be a column for any changes in the line item in dollars and another column for changes as a percentage. It is important to be specific as to why an increase in the budget is needed.

Financial Control and Budget Management

Financial control is a very important part of managing a library budget. The library will annually want to set up a system for keeping track of all expenditures for the library. This is usually done by category, such as salaries, benefits, library materials (adult print, young adult print, juvenile print, audiovisual, e-resources), and supplies. Libraries most often use fund accounting as a way to monitor the budget. *Fund accounting* means that each line has its own fund code so that as bills are received, they are paid and recorded with a particular fund code. Special funds are given their own code so their expenditures can be reported separately, such as a fund for special gifts for children's books. A record of each expenditure must be kept. During the year the budget must be carefully monitored to see that spending is not less or more than expected. It is important to see that the amount spent each month is about one-twelfth of the budget. There may be good reasons this does not hold true, perhaps because of a major expenditure that only occurs once. But it is important to see that spending is occurring at an even pace.

Libraries may do accrual or cash accounting. In accrual accounting, every time a library orders an item it is recorded as an encumbrance. This means that money is set aside for payment of that expense. In accrual accounting it is easy to see what has been spent so that the library does not overspend its budget. Accrual accounting does not allow for changes in prices; therefore, toward the end of the year the library may have to adjust its budget to allow for price changes. In cash accounting, the library records amounts spent as the item is received at the library and the bill paid. This requires monitoring carefully the orders to be sure that the library is not overspending.

During the year, usually monthly, a report is prepared so that every department is aware of how much of the funds that are allocated to them have been spent. By the end of the year most funds should have been spent. The library's funds should be audited annually to make sure everything is accounted for. Libraries may want to follow the accounting guidelines used by the local government and use a local certified public accountant who is knowledgeable about nonprofits.

Dealing with Budget Cuts

Sometimes the library is in a period of time when it can request and receive increases from the local funding agency. But sometimes the reverse is true. Libraries must always be prepared for cuts in their budget. First of all, the library must be clear as to what its core programs and services are so they can be protected from cuts. Some of the budget lines are fixed costs so they cannot be cut. The rest must be carefully evaluated so that the cuts do not damage the library long term. It may mean, for example, working with neighboring libraries to share resources to make the cuts easier to absorb.

Value of Library Service

Many libraries are using a value calculator to show the return on investment to the community. This calculator will provide information on the value of each service and show the value of library programs and services to the community.

Libraries can add their circulation and other numbers such as programs into this calculator and it will produce information about how much the value of these different elements are for the community. For example, an adult book borrowed is valued at $17, reference assistance is valued at $7, and attendance at an adult program is valued at $15.

How valuable is your local library? Use this handy Library Value Calculator (American Library Association n.d.).

Value of Your Library Use		
Input Your Use	**Library Materials & Services**	**Value of Your Use**
	Adult Books Borrowed	$ 0.00
	YA Books Borrowed	$ 0.00
	Children's Books Borrowed	$ 0.00
	Audiobooks Borrowed	$ 0.00

	Interlibrary Loan Requests	$ 0.00
	eBooks Downloaded	$ 0.00
	Magazines Read	$ 0.00
	Newspapers Read	$ 0.00
	Movies Borrowed	$ 0.00
	CDs Borrowed	$ 0.00
	Music Downloaded	$ 0.00
	Meeting Room Use (per hour)	$ 0.00
	Adult Program Attended	$ 0.00
	Young Adult Program Attended	$ 0.00
	Children's Program Attended	$ 0.00
	Museum Passes Borrowed	$ 0.00
	Computer Use (per hour)	$ 0.00
	Database Searches	$ 0.00
	Reference Assistance	$ 0.00

	.	
Calculate the Value of Your Library Use	$ 0.00	
This worksheet has been adapted from the Massachusetts Library Association and Chelmsford Library.		

In summary, preparing and presenting the library budget is a crucial part of the library director's and the board of trustees' work. Having an adequate budget is necessary to run the library effectively. Because most libraries are funded with local tax dollars, the library must be careful to spend the public's money carefully. Library patrons and others will notice if the library spends funds in a less-than-careful manner, so it is important the library can account for all its spending.

Table 6.5. Sample library budget

Revenue	
Tax revenue	4,448,100
Income from fines, printing, photocopying, etc	30,000
Interest	12,000
Misc. income	20,000
State funding	8,000
Total revenue	**4,518,100**
Expenditures	
Salaries	**2,600,000**
Benefits	
Retirement	300,000
FICA/Medicare	198,000
Workers' comp	26,000
Disability insurance	3,500
Long-term disability insurance	7,600
Unemployment insurance	1,000
Health insurance	350,000
Total benefits	**886,100**
Equipment and furniture	**50,000**

Library materials (includes print materials, audio, video, periodicals, digital subscriptions)	**550,000**

Administration

Supplies	40,000
Telephone and postage	55,000
Publicity	45,000
Equipment repairs/service contracts	15,000
Conferences/workshops	20,000
Total administration	**175,000**

Utilities and building

Electric, water, gas	140,000
Building maintenance and supplies	70,000
Insurance	47,000
Total utilities and building	**57,000**

Total expenditures	**$4,518,100**

Discussion Questions

1. What are good reasons for keeping a line-item budget, and what are good reasons for using a program budget?

2. Do you think library budgets tell a story?

Bibliography

American Library Association. n.d. "Library Value Calculator." Accessed December 9, 2020. http://www.ala.org/advocacy/advleg/advocacyuniversity/toolkit/makingthecase/calculator_new.

Hall, Kate, and Kathy Parker. 2019. *The Public Library Director's Toolkit*. Chicago: American Library Association.

Prentice, Ann E. 2011. *Public Libraries in the 21st Century*. Santa Barbara, CA: Libraries Unlimited.

Public Library Association. n.d. "Administration and Leadership: Library Budgets and Funding." Accessed December 9, 2020. http://www.ala.org/pla/resources/tools/directors-managers-administrators/administration-leadership.

COMMUNITY AND CIVIC ENGAGEMENT AND OUTREACH SERVICES

- • Overview and definitions
- • Essential elements of community and civic engagement
- • Guidelines for community and civic engagement
- • Using data
- • Community engagement programs
- • Asset mapping
- • Case studies

Overview and Definitions

Public libraries are open to all people in their community. They are one of the few community institutions that welcome everyone without prejudice or bias. Public librarians try to reach all of their users and potential users in a variety of ways. Some people have grown up using the public library or gravitate to the public library after they have children, while others find their reading material and answers to their questions elsewhere. Librarians have always known that many members of their community do not use the public library. Through the years they have tried many ways to reach out to more residents and encourage them to participate in the public library's programs and services. Librarians have attempted to reach targeted groups, such as members of labor organizations, Spanish-speaking residents, the business community, and older adults, by acquiring materials of interest to a group, planning library programs and services to meet the needs of these groups, and speaking at local meetings. But it was obvious that there were many more groups to reach, that the community was constantly changing, and that perhaps more structure or a different structure was needed. Some attempts at outreach have worked well while others have not. Even successful outreach ventures have often ended when budgets were cut, a grant ended, or the staff person doing the outreach left the library. Most outreach has been limited due to the lack of time that staff had available to move about in their community. But now more than ever libraries are looking for new ways to reach and serve their community. This part of librarianship must be central to library work. This chapter will focus on how libraries can do the planning necessary to reach their community.

Community engagement is the newest iteration of community outreach services. "Community engagement encompasses a variety of approaches whereby public service bodies empower citizens to consider and express their views on how their particular needs are best met" (Rogers and Robinson 2004, 116). It is described as the act of meeting people where they are and building relationships and trust with members of the community, community groups, and community institutions. It is about listening to the community, turning outward, and providing resources, programs, and services to meet their needs. For libraries this means bringing resources and services to people outside the library as well as inside the library. It means connecting them with library and community services, which might include book delivery and programs, both in the library and in other locations, or providing services such as space for a group to hold a meeting in the library. It also means letting the community participate in the library's discussions as to how they develop services and programs for the community. Finally, it means developing partnerships with other community groups. Community engagement needs some structure but must remain flexible since no two situations are the same.

Essential Elements of Community and Civic Engagement

Hui-Yun Sung, Mark Hepworth, and Gillian Ragsdell (2013) defined what they saw as the essential elements of community engagement: belonging, commitment, communication, flexible approach, genuineness, relevance, and sustainability.

- Belonging involves relationship building. It goes two ways so that both the library and the community were involved in discussing library plans.

- Commitment involves emotional engagement. The community must be enthusiastic and bring energy to the library's program and support and trust what the library is doing.

- Communication must be two ways so that the library is listening to what the community is saying that they want and the community is articulating its needs and interests.

- In flexibility the library must show that it can use many different methods to meet community interests and needs. It could be providing surveys and questionnaires from the library to actual participation in planning library programs and services through a Friends of the Library group. The library must determine if on-site programming is best or whether the library needs to go out to the community.

- In genuineness the library must show its authenticity and that it can turn community needs into action.

- In relevance the library must engage the stakeholders and community members and show that they understand what they are saying and take action.

- In sustainability the library must develop a sustainable program as it moves forward. (Sung, Hepworth, and Ragsdell 2013)

Taking all these elements into consideration, the library can move forward confident that it understands and can meet the needs of its community. This is obviously not an easy task and will call for continual work on the part of the library.

Guidelines for Community and Civic Engagement

In our current world there are not many places for people to meet that are open to all and promote social inclusion. The library can be that place where everyone can feel comfortable. Here are some guidelines for how the library staff can begin to get more involved in the community and develop strong relationships, which can lead to more use of the public library:

- Encourage the staff to do research on the community and develop a community profile. Find out the demographics as well as the needs and interests of people in the community. Both formal and informal research is needed. Surveys and focus groups can be used to gather information. For example, it may be determined that many in the community need jobs and do not have good resources for job hunting. This is a place where libraries can help both with information services and programs and can identify community partners who can also assist.

- Find out what resources and services are presently being provided to the community. The library may want to provide resources and services not presently being provided, or it may want to partner with an existing program. For example, there may be another group in the community providing English as a second language classes, so maybe the library can provide additional resources for the program or even space for the group to meet. Another need might be for more technology and technology training. The library can probably provide some of this but might look for other community partners.

- Talk to community leaders and encourage them to make suggestions as to what else the library can do. There might be a need for an advisory group for the library, or the library might want to visit existing community groups and talk with them about services the library could provide.

- Set up community conversations where the ideas of many in the community can be explored. The conversations can be held in the library and in other locations in the community. Encourage the participants in the conversations to talk about what they want to see for their community. What would make the community a better place to live? See what ideas continue to be mentioned. Identify unmet community needs; these could be very specific needs or could just be the need for enrichment.

- Do periodic surveys to find out what the library is doing right and what is missing that the library might be able to do. Sometimes people have ideas for community events, but they never think of the library. So the surveys have to be worded in such a way as to encourage responses that at first may seem not to be something the library can do.

- Send the library staff out into the community. Staff will need time to work outside the library and get to know people, community institutions, and organizations. They must know that this is part of their job and not just an extra when they have a spare minute. The more people in the community see the library staff, the more they will talk to them and share ideas. Begin to explore what the barriers are to using the library.

- Contact institutions and organizations with whom the library might partner, such as the local schools, parks and recreation departments, the local chamber of commerce, and local civic organizations, such as the League of Women Voters and the Lions Club. This will probably mean going to a few meetings and listening to what the group is doing and then thinking about how the library might participate. Promote networking among the local residents and the library.

- Staff can also identify possible organization or institution partners and proceed to set up appointments with them to get to know them. A first meeting may not accomplish everything that the library had hoped for. Patience is required, and follow-up meetings to explore ideas further should be set up.

Through the contacts with local institutions and organizations, the staff can begin to develop ideas for partnerships that will enhance both groups. No community is exactly the same, so the services and programs will be geared to that specific community. One library might want to work with arts and cultural organizations, whereas another might want to work with local health organizations. Partnerships are a way of making the best use of limited local resources, increasing the profile of the library, and finding new sources of expertise and skills.

Community engagement emphasizes the sustainability of services. It makes the community feel that their ideas have been listened to. By listening to the community the library shows its willingness to change and learn. It also develops trust with the community. And, most important, it shows that the library is looking outward.

Using Data

The library must make use of all kinds of data available. Census data is, of course, primary. This is updated now between the ten-year censuses so that community leaders can get a better idea of the composition of their community. Local data is often collected in a community. The local government, the schools, the chamber of commerce, or other local organizations may do a survey focused on a particular part of the population. Sometimes there is also state government data that is useful. Data can uncover some populations that are not using the library or seldom using the library. This will give the library the opportunity to introduce itself to those groups and find out how the library can serve them. Data is so important in planning.

Community Engagement Programs

Heather Reid and Vivian Howard (2016) wrote about a study in Nova Scotia to find out more about opportunities for community engagement in rural public library systems. Some examples of opportunities for community engagement found in these communities were: partnerships with organizations where the library can support the local organization's services and programs, such as working with a community center and in return the organization will refer people to the library; partnerships with local schools, especially to make them aware of the library's early reading programs; and partnerships with health groups, local arts groups, community internet access programs, and local recreation programs. A number of these libraries provided programs on new technology, such as coding, 3D printing, and Lego robotics, since there were very few places where their users could learn this technology. The libraries also visited local farmers' markets, job fairs, and other community events, setting up tents or booths to provide information on the library. They stressed that it was important to identify unmet community needs by listening carefully to the needs of users and nonusers. The libraries especially wanted to find out what the barriers were to nonusers using the public library. Sometimes they found that the barriers were lack of access, so these libraries provided books by mail, homebound deliveries, bookmobiles, and even satellite branches (Reid and Howard 2016).

A branch of the Free Library of Philadelphia had been closed for renovation and was just about to reopen when Hurricane Maria devastated Puerto Rico. This branch was in a neighborhood with many Puerto Ricans, so refugees from the storm began to arrive in the neighborhood as island residents found shelter with their relatives. These refugees needed many services in order to cope in their new surroundings. The library's community organizers who were already in place saw this as an opportunity for the library to assist. They contacted FEMA (Federal Emergency Management Agency) to find out what services were available and how the library could assist. The first thing was to invite the refugees in to help them to fill out FEMA forms on the computers. Volunteers were recruited to help them. The library began to meet on a regular basis with FEMA and other local agencies that were prepared to provide assistance and arranged drop-in hours where people could talk to FEMA, local housing nonprofits, the Philadelphia Housing Authority, and local volunteers. This has even included a free food distribution program at the library. The Free Library of Philadelphia has community organizers in each of their library regions who work in the community and identify needs, often going house to house and informing citizens of library services.

John Ouligian documented using the Harwood philosophy of community engagement at the Youngstown (Ohio) Public Library. This story actually began in 1999, when the Harwood Institute did a report on Youngstown. This report came to the attention of the director and board of trustees of the Youngstown Public Library. The report stated that the community must be the center of the institution's decision-making. It promoted the philosophy of Turning Outward. The library began to invoke this idea by changing their programming and providing more appropriate programming for the community. As they worked more closely with the community, they involved the community more and more. When new branches were being designed, they involved those communities in the planning. When the budget was severely cut, they went to the community and asked them to support a levy to fund the library. It passed. The library has continued to have Community Conversations, which are small-group conversations that give the administration a chance to get to know the community better. As a result, many difficult decisions have been taken to the community to gain their support.

In San Antonio there was a lack of knowledge about computers and a lack of connectivity in some of the housing projects. The library worked with several groups to provide equipment (computers), training, and connectivity for low-income families, seniors, and youth. The computers were supplied by Goodwill, the training was provided by Girls, Inc. and the library and the connectivity was provided by many partners, including Sprint, Google Fiber, AT&T, and Best Buy. The next step was to formalize city support. The library was able to provide hot spots and some laptops. This is an excellent example of the library working together with many groups.

Public libraries have emerged as a place for discussion and conversation. An article in *Public Libraries* showcased the efforts of the Sno-Isle Libraries (Washington state) to use discussion as a means of community engagement. Each year since 2015 the library has asked the community for possible discussion topics for a program entitled "Issues That Matter." The topics suggested have included mental health, drug addition, lack of affordable housing, and homelessness. Each program has local speakers and a moderator. The programs use local resource people and work in partnership with local organizations knowledgeable about the topic under discussion. These partners also help to publicize the programs. The programs aim to provide more than one point of view and a chance for local residents to gain more knowledge of the topic. The library provides a list of resources on each topic—local agencies working on this issue, books, and other educational materials—so the community can continue to learn. The community has also asked for action items, and speakers now provide this too. The library says that this series has provided them with invaluable partnerships with many local organizations (Pratt, Gustafson, and Batdorf 2019).

Other libraries have developed similar programs to engage their communities. Sacramento (California) Public Library developed a "Let's Talk About" series. Each program begins with a panel that provides different but factual points of view on the topic for the evening. There is time for questions from the audience too. The audience is encouraged to continue their conversations with others after the program and to think about how to move from the information to action.

The Pierce County (Washington) Library System hosts a series called "Get Informed. Be Empowered. Join the Conversation." The library sees itself as a facilitator of discussions of current topics. The programs are varied but might include book clubs, informational programs, and opportunities to take action.

Skokie (Illinois) Public Library has developed Civic Lab Pop-Ups. The library offers at least one pop-up topic a month, which is repeated. There are four main types of civic lab topics: topics in the news (e.g., gun violence), basic civic literacy (e.g., how a bill becomes a law), timely topics (e.g., talking about taxes), and news literacy (e.g., what journalism is and what it isn't). The pop-ups include supporting visuals, activities, or conversation starters. A resource handout is provided with credible information on the topic. The idea of the resource list is to provide reputable information on the topic. Each resource listed is annotated. One or two staff members facilitate the pop-up, which lasts sixty to ninety minutes. The library wants the patrons who participate to come to their own conclusions. It is not meant to be an opposing viewpoints program (Koester 2019).

There are many other ways for a public library to engage its community. More than one public library has found that holding naturalization ceremonies at the public library is an excellent way to reach out to new members of their community and their friends and relatives. Linda Osuna and Carol Reich (2019) wrote about holding naturalization ceremonies at the Hillsboro (Oregon) Public Library. The library hosts administrative ceremonies. They explain that there are specific requirements that the library must follow. But they think it is very worthwhile because the library gets lots of publicity from it and local people who may not have used the library are introduced to it. Another public library that hosts naturalization ceremonies is the Memphis Public Library. They also provide an exhibit with information from organizations that new Americans might want to contact.

Asset Mapping

Another approach to community engagement is asset mapping. In this case study, the Halifax (Canada) Public Library staff used asset mapping to find out more about their immigrant community and how they could serve it. They collected information about the community's assets and its needs by talking to individuals and community groups. By collecting this information the library could better understand how to build its resources and services. It is no longer a case of the library trying to figure out what the community needs; rather, the staff has been out in the community and collected information on the assets and needs of the community. The staff talked to immigrant service providers about their programs and the services they provided. They found out both their strengths and assets and their needs. They asked them what role the library could play. The library readily acknowledged that the people in the community were those most knowledgeable of their own strengths and needs. Once the library understood this, it could go forward with its planning (Williment and Jones-Grant 2012).

As a result of the asset mapping, the Halifax Public Library developed a newcomers program called "Opening Doors." It included a community advisory board, multilingual computer classes, a knitting group for immigrant women, an art show of the work of immigrant women, and an immigrants' culture week. The library has developed materials collections in many other languages, recruited multilingual staff, and provided information on the library in other languages.

Case Studies

The Harwood Institute for Public Innovation has worked with the American Library Association on a project entitled "Transforming Communities." This program emphasizes listening to the community through a series of conversations. David Seleb, director of the Oak Park (Illinois) Library, has written about his experiences after going through this program. His library has hosted many community conversations both inside and outside the library. Seleb emphasized that it was important to ask the right questions: "What kind of community do you want to live in? Why is that important to you? What needs to happen? Whom do you trust to do that work?" Seleb described the common themes from their community conversations:

- Diversity, inclusion, equity

- Economy

- Education, literacy

- Health, safety, affordability

Many things have changed at Oak Park Library resulting from this program, such as a librarian of practice model, making space changes, tighter external relationships, empowering families to learn together, and working with users on theme-related title selection. Also resulting from this program, Oak Park Library hired a social worker as a member of the staff. One significant program that they developed was a "continuum of care model for the most vulnerable" in their community, which meant providing a safe space for everyone (Seleb and Kolo 2017).

At the Evanston Public Library in Illinois, a librarian was hired to provide community engagement to the Latino community. This took the form of building relationships with the residents, institutions, and organizations. The librarian looked at the library's mission statement and strategic plan and how those have connected with the Latino community. He also began to build and rebuild connections and partnerships with this community through meetings with groups and individuals and follow-up to the meetings. He identified local and national resources that would be of use to this community.

At the Shaker Heights Public Library in Ohio, community engagement took the form of relationship building, meeting people where they are, and engaging local leadership. The staff recommended moving slowly to build social capital by developing trust. Capacity building and asset mapping were emphasized as well as cultivating relationships with community organizations. The staff realized that the library needs to connect residents with each other and with needed resources and to set attainable goals. As an example of their community engagement, they worked with a theater group that was given space in the library to produce a play based on African American literature. This was a way of attracting a new group of potential users to the library.

The Dallas Public Library in Texas has developed the HELP Desk (Homeless Engagement and Leadership Program). This unique program has developed not only one-to-one assistance to the homeless but also library programs that both involve the homeless and are provided for the homeless and to others as well.

In summary, community engagement continues to be an important part of the life of the public library. The library staff must move out of the library to meet the citizens of their community and learn what they need from the public library. Just serving the users who come to the public library is not enough. For many reasons, others need to know more about the public library and to partake of the library's offerings.

Discussion Questions

1. If you were a new public library director, what steps would you take to increase the library's community engagement?

2. What about community engagement interests you most?

Bibliography

Koester, Amy. 2019. "A Civic Initiative about Information: The Civic Lab at Skokie Public Library." *Public Libraries* 58, no. 4 (July/August): 45–52.

Osuna, Linda, and Carol Reich. 2019. "Welcome to the United States: Naturalization Ceremonies at Your Public Library." *Public Libraries* 58, no. 4 (July/August): 54–59.

Pratt, Charles, Sonia Gustafson, and Kurt Batdorf. 2019. "Issues That Matter: Forums Build Civic Engagement." *Public Libraries* 58, no. 4 (July/August): 35–43.

Reid, Heather, and Vivian Howard. 2016. "Connecting with Community: The Importance of Community Engagement in Rural Public Library Systems." *Public Library Quarterly* 35, no. 3 (July/September): 188–202.

Rogers, B., and Robinson, E. 2004. *The Benefits of Community Engagement: A Review of the Evidence*. London: Home Office.

Seleb, David J., and Jodi Kolo. 2017. "Our Path to Engagement: Learning and Stewardship; The Oak Park Public Library, the American Library Association, and the Harwood Institute." *Public Library Quarterly* 36, no. 2 (June): 123–35.

Sung, Hui-Yun, Mark Hepworth, and Gillian Ragsdell. 2013. "Investigating Essential Elements of Community Engagement in Public Libraries: An Exploratory Qualitative Study." *Journal of Librarianship and Information Science* 45, no. 3 (September): 206–18.

Williment, Kenneth, and Tracey Jones-Grant. 2012. "Asset Mapping at Halifax Public Libraries: A Tool for Beginning to Discover the Library's Role with the Immigrant Community in Halifax." *Partnership: The Canadian Journal of Library and Information Practice and Research*, special section 7 (1): 1–12.

SERVICES TO CHILDREN AND YOUNG ADULTS

Lisa Houde

Lisa Houde is the assistant director of the Rye (New Hampshire) Public Library and a lecturer at San José State University. Prior to her present position, she was the director of youth services.

- Overview and definitions
- Collection development
- Programming
- Professional development and understanding childhood development
- The future of youth services and public libraries

Overview and Definitions

This is an exciting time for librarians/information professionals with the possibilities they have of developing and shifting the role of the library to meet the needs of their communities. Note the use of the term *information professional*; the current shift from the librarian as a keeper of knowledge to an information professional who engages with the community in innovative ways and who acts as a pathway or connector to knowledge and information and facilitates the interactions of members of the community is key to helping create the public library as an anchor in the community. Pam Smith (2018), in Sandra Hirsh's *Information Services Today: An Introduction*, notes that the new information professionals require different skills beyond the ability to simply point to information and oversee the physical circulation of materials. What's needed now is for the library staff to become guides rather than keepers and to be able to "form strong partnerships and relationships, as well as demonstrating empathy and generosity" (Smith 2018, 94); these are among the new competencies required for successful librarianship. Making these community connections enables the information professional to not only rely on his or her own skill set but also utilize community members who can offer their expertise. The stereotypical introverted librarian hiding behind books has shifted to the need for an outgoing, engaging, and interactive professional who links people with books and information, people with technology, people with their own creativity, and people with people. One might here cue the Barbra Streisand song about people who need people being the luckiest people in the world; it's all about personal connections.

Dr. Michael Stephens (2019) echoes and expands on the notion of including an emotional element in library service: "We are the heart of our communities, and that only works because of what the people who run libraries give of themselves. . . . The best librarians make that emotional investment because they believe in the institution and the communities they serve" (41). Stephens, associate professor in the School of Information at San José State University, recently published *Wholehearted Librarianship: Finding Hope, Inspiration, and Balance.* The book's primary message is to embrace these more recent developments in library services and to temper innovation with core values and services in the library—and to do this with heart. While this advice applies to librarianship at all levels of service, it can be especially helpful for youth librarians/information professionals who require an emotional investment in the welfare of their young patrons. Setting the stage for lifelong learning and reading, youth services information professionals can have a significant impact on the lives of the youth they serve.

The public library has transformed from its infancy as merely a repository for books to a burgeoning, vibrant community center for learning, engaging, and connecting people of all ages. From infant story times to teen makerspaces, public libraries have grown to meet the needs of their communities, and youth services has led the way with innovative developments as they have reinvented their images, programs, and services, and have done so perhaps even more than many adult service departments. Essentially, children and teen's needs mirror those of adults, but it's critical that the youth librarian understands the nuances that youth require from their public library.

Youth library service has a storied and complicated history, and only in the past twenty years has it been the focus of research, yet studies that have been conducted report that 50 to 60 percent of public library users are youth (Walter 2003, 574). Clearly, this population requires careful consideration, and services to half of all public library users should therefore be carefully crafted. Let's look at some specifics defining this group.

Youth services are defined as those serving young people from birth to age eighteen, and services are delineated as children's and teen or young adult services. There is a rough breakdown of age levels within the library: baby and toddlers start off the group, and books for this age level include board and picture books; early readers are roughly described as those in grades 2 to 3; middle-grade readers include grades 4 to 6 and are reading chapter books; and teen readers include students in grades 7 through 12. There is some disagreement about the moniker for this last age group, whether they're referred to as young adults or teens; for the purposes of this chapter, young people aged twelve to eighteen will be referred to as teens. A brief overview of library services to these teens and their younger peers will help inform innovative library offerings currently being explored.

In its infancy in the 1800s, public library service to children entailed the education and development of the young mind with the idea that children required guidance as they grew into contributing members of society; librarians were often seen as censors for children's reading materials, supplying only those books that would make them better people and citizens. As the public library developed in America in 1850 and the American Library Association (ALA) formed in 1876, attention to library service for young people grew. According to ALA websites on the history of its organizations, the Association for Library Service to Children (ALSC) was officially approved as a division of ALA in 1941, after undergoing several transformations as a youth services organization that began as early as 1901. YALSA, the Young Adult Library Services Association, was formally organized in 1957, after a major restructuring of divisions of youth services within the ALA took place. Primary offerings of these groups included providing lists of age-appropriate books, offering guidelines for serving these age groups, and providing suggestions for displays, conference sessions, and workshops for youth librarians.

Realizing that youth services is a rather recent development in history, the vast transformations that have taken place, especially with the rapid advances in technology, and the face of providing library service that meets the needs of the community have advanced exponentially. Beginning with the traditional concept of the library as a place to simply find books; moving to a discussion about programming, intellectual freedom, and censorship; on to professional development for the library; and then to the new approach to the library as a community anchor, we'll examine core services as well as nontraditional offerings through the tempered eye of balancing core library offerings with innovations, while making sure to remain true to the heart of librarianship.

Figure 8.1. A story time program is in progress at the Ames Free Public Library. Their programs are a mainstay of public libraries. *Ames Free Library of Easton, Massachusetts.*

Collection Development

For a librarian, nothing is more satisfying than connecting a person with just the right book: the look of wonder on the reader's face and the enthusiasm of engagement—it just doesn't get better than that. For a youth librarian, this satisfaction can be even more cherished as helping children and teens find books that connect with them often informs their reading habits for a life-time. Consider the young reader of the Harry Potter series who loved them so much they have moved on to other titles; countless caregivers have commented to me that J. K. Rowling's work was a springboard for making their children voracious readers. Not everyone loves fantasy, however, so curating a youth collection for the entire community is complicated; there is no "one size fits all" book. This overview will focus on the traditional and nontraditional approaches to collection development.

Before discussing purchasing books and other materials, the youth librarian should familiarize himself or herself with the library's collection development policy. This document serves several purposes: It provides a guide on how materials will be collected and retained, and eventually whether they will be deaccessioned or withdrawn, but it will also serve as a resource if books are challenged for removal; this is especially pertinent to youth services as the ALA's annual list of books challenged, restricted, removed, or banned primarily consists of books for youth. As a point of reference, in 2018, 483 books were challenged or banned, and the top eleven of those books were youth titles and included picture books, graphic novels, and teen titles. Taking a snapshot of books listed from 2014 to 2018, and categorizing crossover books as adult books, there were still thirty-eight out of fifty-one listed top-ten titles that belong in the category of children or teen literature. Clearly, a policy protecting the library and acting as a resource in the case of an attempted ban or challenge is a critical document. If no collection development policy exists, it's important to work with library administration to develop a clear and concise policy that includes specific steps to take when a challenge presents itself. It's interesting to note that despite the censor's attempts to restrict access to materials he or she finds objectionable, bringing them even more into the limelight by publicly challenging them has the reverse effect of making them even more desirable to read; the stereotypical rebellious teen lives on in teens and adults! The American Library Association's Office for Intellectual Freedom works to ensure access to materials on all subjects without restriction and provides updated information on banned or challenged books as well as any news pertaining to the concept of intellectual freedom. For current discussions on this topic, find frequently updated posts on the *Intellectual Freedom Blog*. An excellent resource for the library or just as a general interest resource is the *Intellectual Freedom Manual* (9th edition), published in 2015; it contains documents and policy statements of the ALA, court cases related to intellectual freedom in understandable language, advocacy for intellectual freedom for minors, and much more.

Prior to addressing details, it's important to note that the term *collection* refers only loosely to the actual books a library holds. Today's library offers materials in multiple and varied formats, including electronic resources, digital collections, audio and music CDs, streaming platforms like Hoopla, DVDs, and magazines both physical and available electronically, and one might even check out a sewing machine, toys, puzzles, games, fishing gear—really, the sky is the limit. These traditional and nontraditional holdings vary from library to library and cater to the needs of the communities they serve. For now, we'll look at physical book collections and how they should be carefully considered.

Library budgets often inform the number and type of materials that a library might offer its patrons, but a carefully built library collection will nonetheless provide community-specific materials. It's important to note that a collection of materials needs to include books and materials for *all* community members. Too often, particular demographics are not considered, or are mistakenly or even deliberately overlooked. Consider materials for all people that include multiple definitions of family, a wide range of religious and political viewpoints, and culturally diverse people, ethnicities, and sexual and gender orientations. It's important that youth librarians get a real sense of the communities and patrons they serve; connecting with local schools, networking with fellow librarians in adjacent towns, and working with public and private recreational organizations will help provide a clearer picture of community needs.

Standard books for the very young include board books for babies and picture books for toddlers, preschoolers, and younger school-age children. Materials for this age group feature developmentally appropriate picture books for both the younger reader and more advanced early readers; in this collection, as for every age level, include a diverse body of engaging materials in which multiple cultures, ethnicities, religious perspectives, and so forth are represented. In this area, note that the librarian will be assisting both caregivers and their young people with finding the books they need.

Books for emerging readers can be perplexing as they are categorized by reading level differently from one publisher to another. Become familiar with the library's collection and recommend titles based on their accessibility for the appropriate age group.

A strong collection is weeded aggressively! This may seem counterintuitive, but the deaccession or "weeding" process is critical to keeping the collection vibrant and pertinent. It may be painful to remove beloved titles, but if the community doesn't need or have interest in them, they must go. Likewise, outdated informational books—for example, keeping up with Pluto's status as a planet or not—need to reflect current and updated information.

Consider using the H. W. Wilson Core Collection reference books created for and by librarians; these titles function as purchase guides, as help in readers' advisory, cataloging support, and collection maintenance: *Children's Core Collection*, *Middle and Junior High Core Collection*, *Young Adult Core Collection*, *Senior High Core Collection*, and *Graphic Novels Core Collection*. Each lengthy book covers respective age groups, and the graphic novel collection covers all age groups along with adult graphic novels. Graphic novels are growing increasingly popular, and this reference book is an invaluable guide to creating a core collection. These books are an important resource for the weeding process, but the librarian ultimately knows her or his own community best. The primary challenge to maintaining a vibrant collection is understanding the balance of providing popular titles and those that may challenge the reader and broaden their perspectives.

An excellent outreach opportunity for the public librarian is to consult with teachers concerning materials students may need, and this will further inform the librarian's collection development. Collaborating with schools and including materials in the collection that assist students with project assignments in addition to materials geared for pleasure reading builds community connections.

Remember that the primary service is for youth, but many libraries opt to build collections for caregivers that are housed in the youth department. In terms of accessibility, it makes sense to have materials for caregivers in this area. Developing a broad range of titles in this collection would necessarily include books for new caregivers, items that help caregivers understand the developmental needs of children at all ages, and any title that will help caregivers navigate the upbringing of children. Keeping this collection current and updated can be overlooked, but it is critical that the collection represents recent research and pertinent topics.

Traditional resources for youth collection development include three major professional publications: *The Horn Book Magazine*, *School Library Journal*, and *Voice of Youth Advocates* (*VOYA*). Other publications that feature reviews for youth materials include *Booklist*, *Publishers Weekly*, and *Book Page*. Although in the past few years major publishing houses have begun to publish more diverse titles, it's important to reach beyond those major publishing houses to independent publishers for a wider range of materials; the librarian will need to dig a bit deeper to locate independent publishers and their offerings. Additionally, consulting personal blogs and book reviews, especially those of middle grade or teen readers, creates an authentic snapshot of what youth are reading and enjoying. For example, teenreads.com offers monthly picks and reviews derived from teen contributors. The blog *I'm Here. I'm Queer. What the Hell Do I Read?* offers more book reviews for young LGBTQ (lesbian, gay, bisexual, transgender, and queer/questioning) readers than can be imagined. Debbie Reese's *American Indians in Children's Literature* blog is a compendium of information on authors and books published in that framework. While many more diverse titles are being published as mentioned, there is still a gap in publishing books featuring indigenous peoples of this continent. Making a concerted effort to locate and purchase materials representing all people is the primary function of a public library's collection development work.

Finally, another resource for collection development is annual national book awards. The Caldecott, Newbery, Belpré, Coretta Scott King, Sibert, and Geisel awards are a few of the books chosen yearly for children by committees of the ALA. Included among the ALA awards for young adults are the Morris Award, the Printz Award, Great Graphic Novels, and YALSA's Best Fiction for Young Adults. Additional awards include the Rainbow Book List and the Stonewall Awards created by the Gay, Lesbian, Bisexual, and Transgender Round Table, with suggestions for all ages, and the Schneider Winner List, which honors authors or illustrators of books that express the disability experience of children or teens.

While award winners provide nice resource lists for purchase, youth in every community may or may not be interested in these titles; it's been noted that some teens balk at the books chosen for them and instead gravitate toward titles that their peers are reading. Balancing popular and literary titles is tricky, and knowing patrons is ultimately the best way to determine how to build the youth collection; therefore, once again, reaching out to the community and participating in community events provide value and insight into learning about just what the patrons in the library's area need.

Finally, a youth librarian must know the collection not only through reading widely in varied genres but also by conducting a survey of the materials in its holdings. Are there books for all people in the community? Are all genres covered? Does the library hold any award-winning titles, and if so, what are the circulation statistics on those books? Filling gaps in the collection and running circulation reports are essential to maintaining a strong collection.

Figure 8.2. A children's program at the Wallingford Public Library is well received. *Courtesy of the Wallingford Public Library, Connecticut.*

Programming

Like collection development, programming has undergone seismic shifts in terms of what is offered and how the success of program offerings is measured. It was once enough to simply provide a head count as evidence of a program's success. In today's library, understanding whether a person has been changed in some way, whether needs or expectations were met, or whether something new was learned can be a more valuable measurement that can lead to better funding as well as staff and patron buy-in. Before getting to those assessment tools, though, let's look at programming for youth and how traditional programming that's still being offered is defined.

Service to babies and toddlers falls under the enormous changes in programming offerings; in the past, caregivers brought their children along to the library as they filled their own library needs. Today, the library offers baby lap-sit story times, baby yoga, toddler story times, and other programming created especially for toddlers and preschoolers, and summer reading programs are designed for all ages. Early literacy support offerings, such as the award-winning *Mother Goose on the Loose* program that focuses on the developmental literacy needs of babies through repetitive rhymes, puppets, songs, music, and movement, use research-based data to address the needs of the whole child (https://mgol.net). Baby yoga programs help to build and solidify the bond between the caregiver and baby by giving them a designated time each week to connect through focused interactive yoga poses using songs and rhymes.

Libraries have traditionally offered and continue to offer all manner of programs for school-aged children, from superhero parties to Harry Potter book nights and chess clubs, ice cream tastings, trivia sessions, and cupcake wars. The imagination knows no bounds when it comes to the diversity of programs that can be offered. It's important that librarians are sensitive to programming offered under the guises of gender—programming that might appeal more to girls and those that appeal more to boys—because all genders should feel welcome to join in all library programs. As in all library services, the success of the library's programming depends on how well the librarians know their community, but it's important to be bold and creative to see just what works. There will be failures (e.g., when programs are planned very carefully and no one shows up); by viewing this as an opportunity to learn more about the community, it's less a failure than a tool for future use, although it could also indicate that it's more about timing and outreach than the program itself. Many young people engage in after-school activities, and knowledge of the school's after-school programs and sports opportunities as well as community events will help inform how the library might schedule programs or fill gaps in what's being offered.

Teen programming also includes a wide range of options. What is of more importance here is that in order to attain teen buy-in for these programs, teens themselves need to be included in planning and implementation. Teen advisory boards offer an excellent opportunity for teens to become civic minded and have ownership of their public library. Activities at these board meetings can range from assisting in collection development and program planning to simply providing a social time for teens to gather and play literary-themed games. Try book spine poetry, having teens find books with faces on the cover and photographing advisory board members with the books in front of their faces, or trivia nights based on popular titles. Programs for all teens might include movie marathons or even multigenerational programs in which teens assist elders in using technology. As in school-aged children's programming, there is no limit to the ways the librarian can draw teens to the library for programs.

To ensure attendance, food can be a big draw. Focusing programs around food—literary cake contests, or making mini muffin pizzas, for example—will help with attracting patrons to programs, but for successful programs like book clubs, book-to-reel nights, and even those teen advisory board meetings, offering pizza or dessert is highly recommended. Food can also play a vital role or be the sole focus of the program, such as having Harry Potter–themed treats at a Harry Potter movie marathon. To give everyone a chance to contribute to a program, seeking the help of caregivers or teens themselves to spread the task of providing food is helpful; using sign-up

Figure 8.3. A child is reading to a dog, a way of strengthening the child's reading ability. *Courtesy of the Wallingford Public Library, Connecticut.*

sheets will again help with buy-in, and participants will have ownership in the program. A librarian might even use food as an "entry fee" to an event, which will help ensure everyone pitches in and there's a good assortment of offerings.

Librarians have become educational partners for their patrons. While not an official teacher, the librarian's role in instructional learning is an integral part of today's library. As mentioned at the onset of this section, early literacy programs for babies reflect just that kind of instructional design that's becoming more prevalent in the library. Along with early literacy is literacy for the entire family; whether it's English as a second language, wordless books for challenged readers, or just offering opportunities for educational experiences, the librarian's role is shifting from an information provider to a facilitator.

The youth librarian offers homework assistance, likely dabbles or delves deeply into makerspaces, provides career and trade preparation, and offers information on college preparation as well. In terms of the trendy and growing makerspace or communal creative space, this phenomenon of the public library as a maker "lab" of sorts in which to experiment and create using technology and hand crafts is ubiquitous. In fact, it's grown so rapidly in popularity that assessment tools for the program are unable to keep up.

What, exactly, is a makerspace, and how does the library measure the success of the program? According to Makerspaces.com (2019),

> A makerspace is a collaborative work space inside a school, library or separate public/private facility for making, learning, exploring and sharing that uses high tech to no tech tools. These spaces are open to kids, adults, and entrepreneurs and have a variety of maker equipment including 3D printers, laser cutters, CNC machines, soldering irons and even sewing machines.

Even without high-tech tools, the public library can call itself a makerspace by including crafting and sewing projects, beading, and knitting—virtually anything that produces an object and requires learning how to create that object might be deemed a makerspace.

According to a 2019 *School Library Journal* article, in Boulder, Colorado, the public library offers an award-winning internship for underserved youth in which they create projects that feed directly to the betterment of their community (Keasler 2019). In September 2019, the Boulder Public Library held an internship program in which underserved youth were paid in gift cards in the makerspace they called BLDG 62; they were charged with the following: make something to improve the lives of people who are visually impaired. Two of these youth created two board games for visually impaired people and are now working to have their games published, and both interns plan to pursue engineering degrees. This innovative program clearly illustrates how the library has expanded to meet the needs of its community by providing "out of the box" opportunities for patrons.

Partnerships with local businesses and other professionals in the community can also provide a wealth of programming opportunities. In Rye, New Hampshire, the public library partnered with a nearby bead store in which the librarian learned various beading techniques at no charge from the store owner and then taught the project to teens. In turn, teens were given information about the bead store and shopped there to make more beading projects, increasing the store's business. This is a win-win-win model that works. Libraries have also held "how-to" fairs in which many of the community's professionals demonstrate how to effectively create or perform a task relevant to their business. Included in these fairs is a wide range of topics, including dog obedience training, how to crochet, the instructions on fermenting and its benefits, fire safety, foster parenting, basic automobile care, house painting techniques—and the list goes on. Establishing community partners also creates mechanisms for resources assistance, including requiring food donations as an "entry fee" for library programs. What is needed in the nearby homeless shelter? Determining the answer to this question as well as researching the services available in the community will enhance the library's offerings and provide awareness and much-needed resources.

For programming ideas, the librarian can consult Pinterest or the ALA website on programming, and even conducting a simple Google search for "library programs" will yield infinite possibilities.

Professional Development and Understanding Childhood Development

Serving young patrons, the youth librarian should have at least a rudimentary awareness of childhood development and its stages as well as keeping current with trends and cultural developments. Gretchen Kaser Corsillo (2015) on the Public Library Association website, which is a part of the ALA, outlines ten essential key qualifications and areas of knowledge for youth librarians:

1. Current trends in early literacy practices and education.

2. The importance of the reference interview.

3. Understanding the needs of all levels of readers.

4. An awareness of pop culture.

5. Management and networking skills.

6. How to talk to children.

7. Technological know-how.

8. How to be a creative problem solver.

9. Time management.

10. How to promote library services.

All ten of the above key points are valuable, and each requires a particular skill set. Let's touch on a few. To begin, the first point, to stay current with educational practices, requires an understanding of the common core and current pedagogy, which, as Kaser Corsillo notes, will help with patron service as well as collection development. Additionally, reaching out to schools will build a strong collaboration.

The *reference interview* referred to in the second point is the term used to help a person find the materials they're looking for. Getting the question from a teen, "Do you have any good books?" can be daunting, but a carefully crafted interaction can be helpful in getting teens the books they want and will also dictate whether the teens will be back for help in the future. The Reference and User Services Association (RUSA) of the ALA provides helpful guidelines for the reference interview. Kay Ann Cassell and Uma Hiremath (2018) outline the five elements of the reference interview as: approachability, interest, listening/inquiring, searching, and follow-up (26, 27).

Some librarians find the actual term reference interview off-putting in its formality, but reframing that concept as a readers' advisory conversation may be helpful. Cindy Orr, in Cassell and Hiremath (2018), presents Joyce Saricks assertion that "thinking of this contract with a patron as informal may take away some of the pressure that makes many librarians think of the RA [readers' advisory] question as the scariest reference question there is. Informality leads to more listening, and give-and-take, allowing for a better transaction, and it encourages the reader to come back for another conversation" (292–93).

Understanding reading levels listed as the third point as well as comprehending developmental stages for youth provide a solid foundation on which to recommend titles and meet youth "where they are." The Child Development Institute (2019) offers the following breakdown of developmental stages: babies are classified as being from birth to two years old, toddlers are comprised of children eighteen months to three years old, preschoolers include three- to six-year-olds, school-age children are between the ages of six and twelve, and teenagers and adolescents are youth aged thirteen to eighteen. Texts that can help the librarian comprehend developmental stages for youth include *The Youth Development Handbook: Coming of Age in American Communities*, edited by Stephen Hamilton and Mary Hamilton (2004).

An awareness of pop culture will, of course, provide common ground for youth and the librarian and will inform the librarian's ability to interact with children—helping them to communicate in a relatable way.

A final comment on these key points is the importance of carefully scheduled and a carefully adhered to administrative schedule that includes library promotion, the ability to creatively solve problems, and the ability to manage time well. This just makes sense in any position, and these skills benefit the youth librarian, but a bit more information on library promotion would be helpful here.

An information professional has a great idea for a program—but how to attract patrons? How about attaining a budget for programming and collection development? For successful program attendance, community and administration buy-in and a healthy circulation of the library's youth collection are needed. The librarian must employ "shameless self-promotion" and must act as an advocate for youth.

To begin, the librarian needs buy-in from the administration, and that frequently involves providing measurable outcomes in library programming—not just an attendance tally. Eliza Dresang, Melissa Gross, and Leslie Holt (2006) offer a tested strategy for program planning and determining outcomes in *Dynamic Youth Services through Outcome-Based Planning and Evaluation*. The strategic plan employs designing programming around outcomes that are informed by community research and market analysis, and by using this format, the library will gain the funding needed as well as patron involvement and interest. It's important to note that if a public library has a strategic plan in place, aligning programming with the mission of the library and its strategic plan will further the advocacy for youth programming.

While Cecilia Freda (2007) presents her argument for advocacy for school library programming, the same concepts she presents also apply to public library programming; she states, "What makes libraries particularly primed for advocacy is that so much of what goes on in them is invisible to the public eye. If our public thinks that circulating books is all we do and all that we have to do, then how can we expect them to be impressed by our influence within the school community?" (49). She makes a good point here, and public librarians need to be proactive in informing the community of what goes on within its walls. Social media, school newsletters to caregivers, and weekly emails to patrons—all of these tools assist in not only showing the value of the library to stakeholders, but also furthering the library's efforts to provide pertinent programming and its intrinsic value; additionally, they all help advertise the library's programming as well as available books. For more ideas on advertising programs and the collection, combine book and program promotion in an annual outreach event at schools to inform students of the upcoming summer reading program as well as book-talking state award nominated titles. Here again, searching for library promotion on the ALA website will yield countless more advertising options.

Frequent perusal of the ALA website's many resources will help the librarian remain current and appraised of technological advances and innovative ways to view library service. YALSA's *Journal of Research on Libraries and Young Adults* is a refereed journal presenting topics on young adults and libraries; subscribing to this publication is an excellent way to remain current on the latest in services for teens. Likewise, the quarterly publication *Children and Libraries* published by the ALSC provides research and educational updates for the librarian working with school-aged children. Professional development is critical to keeping library services relevant and to serving patrons' ever-changing needs.

Finally, about those many professional organizations mentioned in this chapter—depending on the budget for professional development, at the very least, belonging to local regional or state organizations is vital. The state's library and library associations are a good resource to determine what organizations are available locally. If budgets permit, belonging to national organizations and chapters or roundtables within those organizations can be

Figure 8.4. Children's rooms in public libraries are ideal for families to spend time together reading and talking. *Fat Camera/(E+) via Getty Images.*

incredibly beneficial. The key is to seek out updated information on library services frequently.

The Future of Youth Services and Public Libraries: Anchors, Passages, and Possibilities

There's no doubt that we are living in an information age, and keeping up with the rapid cycling of technology is daunting. Taking part in local and state programs and working toward a graduate degree in information technology is an effective way to network and stay current. With all this technology, though, is the librarian even needed? With the advent of Google and other search engines, isn't the role of the librarian obsolete? How have libraries remained relevant in this technologically advanced age? Indeed, as outlined in the opening paragraphs of this chapter, the role of the librarian has expanded from simply providing information to assisting patrons with finding, evaluating, and using that information successfully themselves and for bringing threads of the community together in innovative ways. The ability to evaluate what is found online is critical, and information professionals have expanded their roles to include this vital service. In addition to this expansion of the job description, it's incumbent on the librarian to further determine specific library needs within their communities—especially with the lightning speed at which technology is developing and changing. What do youth require concerning information, and how can libraries help fill any gaps in their services?

Additionally, beyond the library's role as a provider of internet services, the concept of community anchor has elevated libraries from the potential of becoming obsolete to becoming a critical resource. Susan Hildreth, in the foreword to Kathleen Campana and Elizabeth Mills's (2019) book *Create, Innovate, and Serve*, states that

> the important role that libraries play in providing access to public computing has been well-documented, and the inclusion of libraries with schools and hospitals as on-ramps to the information superhighway has lifted libraries from their previous "nice to have" status to "need to have"—they are essential for healthy communities. Yet the public library's role as community anchor reaches far beyond supplying high-speed broadband to creating a platform that facilitates people acting individually and in groups in support of knowledge and community. (25)

Hildreth further asserts that library service is focused on four areas that expand the library's role from information center to include a broader range of services: "Libraries advance solutions to their communities' most difficult problems by providing safe places for the community to gather, centers for community vitality, a connecting point to community services, and a venue for lifelong learning" (Hildreth 2019, 25). Campana and Mills offer an invaluable resource for children's and youth programming and a fresh and innovative perspective on providing youth services that touches deeply on the need for libraries to reexamine themselves and their role in their communities. From addressing issues of diversity, library transformation, outreach, and advocacy to providing concrete programming suggestions and well-researched theory, *Create, Innovate, and Serve* divides resources into those for young children, middle childhood, and the teen years. It's among the best offerings for addressing the needs of a burgeoning and vibrant library operating as an anchor in the community, and it specifically informs youth services in relation to the library as that community anchor.

For some final remarks on the pioneering journey of library services today, Smith (2018) observes that skills needed for success in our new technologically advanced age require more than simply "pouring information into students' heads, then testing and moving on to more information. Success in today's world requires the ability to problem-solve, collaborate, and communicate in a myriad of formats (written, verbal, and digital). The four key skills are communication, collaboration, critical thinking, and creativity" (101). This chapter has outlined how those necessary skills might be supported and developed by today's public library, and youth are at the heart of focus as the information professional assists young people in these areas by communicating, collaborating, and thinking critically and creatively themselves as they assess the work and focus of the public library as an anchor in the community.

As a final comment on youth services in the library, librarians have always been on the forefront of innovation and radical thinking—always expanding on the processing and dissemination of ideas. Canadian Peter McLeod, quoted in *Wholehearted Librarianship*, used the term "radicals with heart" to describe librarians (Stephens 2019, 54). As public libraries expand their boundaries of service, keeping the concerns and needs of patrons in mind, having the heart to connect with them, and having the radical notion of connecting them with one another in new ways form the definition of today's librarian and of today's public library as a community anchor.

Discussion Questions

1. What do you think are the most important parts of youth services?

2. What is one new idea you'd like to try in a children's or young adult space?

Bibliography

American Library Association (ALA). 2004. "The Freedom to Read Statement." Accessed September 24, 2019. http://www.ala.org/advocacy/intfreedom/freedom-readstatement.

———. 2018. "American Library Association Names Top 11 Challenged Books of 2018." Accessed September 24, 2019. https://bannedbooksweek.org/american-library-association-names-top-11-challenged-books-of-2018.

———. 2019a. "Brief History of the Young Adults Services Division." Accessed October 2, 2019. http://www.ala.org/yalsa/aboutyalsa/history/briefhistory.

———. 2019b. "History." Accessed October 2, 2019. http://www.ala.org/aboutala/history.

———. 2019c. "Recommended Reading." Accessed October 2, 2019. http://libguides.ala.org/recommended-reading/home.

———. 2019d. "Top Ten Most Challenged Books List." Accessed October 2, 2019. http://www.ala.org/advocacy/bbooks/frequentlychallengedbooks/top10.

Association for Library Service to Children. 2019. "ALSC History." Accessed October 2, 2019. http://www.ala.org/alsc/aboutalsc/historyofalsc.

Campana, Kathleen, and J. Elizabeth Mills, eds. 2019. *Create, Innovate, and Serve: A Radical Approach to Children's and Youth Programming*. Chicago: ALA Neal-Schuman.

Cassell, Kay Ann, and Uma Hiremath. 2018. *Reference and Information Services: An Introduction*, 4th ed. Chicago: American Library Association/Neal Schuman.

Child Development Institute. 2019. "The Ages and Stages of Child Development." Accessed October 3, 2019. https://childdevelopmentinfo.com/ages-stages/#gs.79doqj.

Dresang, Eliza T., Melissa Gross, and Leslie Edmonds Holt. 2006. *Dynamic Youth Services through Outcome-Based Planning and Evaluation*. Chicago: American Library Association.

Freda, Cecilia. 2007. "Promoting Your Library Program: Getting the Message Out." *Knowledge Quest* 36, no. 1 (September/October): 48.

Garcia, Michelle. 2019. "'Make America Straight Again' Pastor Calls for LGBTQ+ Executions." *Out*. Accessed October 3, 2019. https://www.out.com/news/2019/6/12/make-america-straight-again-pastor-calls-lgbtq-executions.

Hildreth, Susan. 2019. "The Library as Community Anchor: An Opening Perspective." In *Create, Innovate, and Serve: A Radical Approach to Children's and Youth Programming*, edited by Kathleen Campana and J. Elizabeth Mills. Chicago: ALA Neal-Schuman.

Hirsh, Sandra, ed. 2018. *Information Services Today: An Introduction*, 2nd ed. Lanham, MD: Rowman & Littlefield.

Houde, Lisa. 2018. *Serving LGBTQ Teens: A Practical Guide for Librarians*. Lanham, MD: Rowman & Littlefield.

Kaser Corsillo, Gretchen. 2015. "Ten Things a Children's Librarian Needs to Know." Public Libraries Online. Accessed October 3, 2019. http://publiclibrariesonline.org/2015/01/ten-things-a-childrens-librarian-needs-to-know.

Keasler, Christina. 2019. "Internship Makes an Impact: Colorado Teens Use Makerspace to Create Accessible Board Games." *School Library Journal* 65 (8): 20–21.

Makerspaces.com. 2019. "What Is a Makerspace?" Accessed October 2, 2019. https://www.makerspaces.com/what-is-a-makerspace.

Mother Goose on the Loose. n.d. "Why MGOL?" Accessed October 5, 2019. https://mgol.net.

Public Library Association. n.d. "Programming and Summer Reading." Accessed October 2, 2019. http://www.ala.org/pla/resources/tools/youth-services/programming-summer-reading.

Robinson, Tracy. 2016. "Overcoming Social Exclusion in Public Library Services to LGBTQ and Gender Variant Youth." *Public Library Quarterly* 35 (3): 161–74. doi: 10.1080/01616846.2016.1210439.

Rye Public Library Board of Trustees. 2014. "Rye Public Library Circulation Policy." Accessed October 3, 2019. https://www.dropbox.com/sh/vgsnrccgoaq5ycb/AAD-PbU1y2ariiEw6hkxJohza?dl=0&preview=Circulation+Policies.pdf.

Smith, Pam. 2018. "Community Anchors for Lifelong Learning: Public Libraries." In *Information Services Today: An Introduction*, 2nd ed., edited by Sandra Hirsh (94–105). Lanham, MD: Rowman & Littlefield.

Stephens, Michael. 2019. *Wholehearted Librarianship: Finding Hope, Inspiration, and Balance*. Chicago: American Library Association.

Walter, Virginia A. 2003. "Public Library Service to Children and Teens: A Research Agenda." *Library Trends* 51 (4): 571–89.

Whelan, Debra Lau. 2009. "A Dirty Little Secret." *School Library Journal* 55 (2): 26–30. Accessed October 5, 2019. https://search.ebscohost.com.

Wilson, H. W. n.d. "Core Collections." Accessed October 5, 2019. https://www.hw-wilsoninprint.com/core_collections.php.

SERVICES TO ADULTS
AND GROUPS OF ADULTS

- Overview and definitions
- History
- Guidelines for developing adult services
- Community survey and needs assessment
- Services to individual adults
- Services to groups
- Services to rural areas
- New and interesting services

Overview and Definitions

Adult services includes all individual adults and groups of adults. Adults are usually defined as persons over twenty-one years old, and there are a number of adult generations to serve. The silent generation was born prior to the end of World War II, the baby boomers were born between 1946 and 1964, those in Generation X were born between 1965 and 1980, the millennials were born between 1981 and 1996, and those in

Generation Z were born after 1997. All these generations have their own life experiences and their own interests and ideas. Adult services includes

- providing information, including the development of collections for adults for recreational reading and for formal and independent learning,

- providing reference service and readers' advisory service,

- providing information literacy, including orientation to the library for individuals and groups,

- providing education, including formal classes and programs, and

- developing a wide variety of services and programs tailored to meet the needs of the adults and groups of adults in a particular community.

Programming and services are an ever-expanding part of adult services as librarians embark on new and creative ways to serve their communities.

Because adults are such a large group to serve, libraries often try to divide them into more manageable groups, as discussed in this chapter. Reaching out to adults who are not accustomed to using public libraries is an important part of a public library's challenge. Many are not aware of what the library offers. So as public libraries expand their programs and services, they begin to add new library users. This chapter explores collections, programs, and services that are aimed at all or part of the adult population.

History

When public libraries began, they only served adults. They circulated books, had reading rooms, and provided lectures and courses in conjunction with the lyceum movement. Late in the nineteenth century (1876), reference service was developed followed by readers' advisory service. Children's services were introduced at the beginning of the twentieth century. (See chapter 8 for more information on children's services.) Early in the twentieth century public libraries began to serve the many immigrants who needed to learn English and were eager to read and borrow books and have a quiet place to read. In branches of large cities, book deposit collections were set up to better serve the people. Services to hospitals followed with the advent of World War I.

Outreach service to rural communities that lacked library services were also developed. Bookmobiles were on the road by the 1920s as well as deposit collections. During the Roosevelt era, the Works Progress Administration (1935–1943) was responsible for funding new public libraries and renovating and repairing others, among other contributions. After World War II, public libraries reached out to refugees.

Adult services was first under the umbrella of adult education. It was recognized by the American Library Association (ALA) with the establishment of the ALA Office of Adult Education in 1952. The Adult Services Division (ASD) was established in 1957. This division was "responsible for those library services designed to provide continuing educational, recreational and cultural development for adults" (Reference and User Services Association [RUSA] n.d.). It was formed out of an ALA interest in adult education as well as readers' advisory services. Other interests of this division were services to such groups as the aging and labor and unions, reading improvement, adult literacy, and programs in the library. The first "Guidelines for Library Services to Adults" was adopted by the division in 1966, with a more developed set of guidelines in 1970. Two projects of the division were "Reading for an Age of Change," which consisted of ten bibliographic essays designed to recommend reading for college graduates, and "Literacy Activities in Public Libraries: A Report of a Study of Services to Adult Illiterates." Out of this report came reading lists for adults who were just learning to read. ASD remained a separate division until 1996 when ASD and the Reference Services Division (RSD) were merged to become RUSA. Today we find some committees in RUSA that have continued since ASD, such as the Notable Books Council and committees on services to labor and unions and on services to the aging.

Guidelines for Developing Adult Services

Planning for adult services is a good way to begin. Here are some steps that can be taken:

- Do a community analysis
- Collect local data, such as demographic information and information about local organizations and agencies
- Compile the information

- Start with developing services for one of the larger groups in the community

- Think about finding a partner organization or institution to join the service development

- Test out the ideas with members of the group that the library wants to reach

- Be open to other ideas or a modification of the program developed

Community Survey and Needs Assessment

Determining the needs of adults in the community is a challenging task. Libraries use several methods and compile the results. One method would be a community survey. This is a fairly brief questionnaire that can be added to the library's website and/or handed out in the library. This survey will provide some basic information about the needs and interests of adults in the community. Further information can be collected by visiting local groups and organizations. Conducting focus groups and interviews are other ways to gain information about adults. Conducting focus groups requires identifying small groups of people to meet with a facilitator and discuss some particular aspect of services to adults. Focus groups can be conducted in the library or out in the community. Interviews can also be done. There should be a plan for interviews as to who should be interviewed and a list of questions developed. Getting out into the community is very important if the library is going to collect information from groups of people who do not use the library often and whose needs remain in the community's neighborhoods. No matter what survey methods are used, the information should be collected and presented in a manner that makes it easy to understand.

Services to Individual Adults

Most services for adults in a public library are available for all adults who wish to take advantage of them. These services include reference/information service, readers' advisory services, educational and recreational programs, and the collections.

Reference service aims to provide information and to answer questions posed by library patrons. It can be face-to-face or by telephone, email, chat, texting, or social media. Email, chat, texting, and social media such as Facebook and Twitter are newer services offered by the library and are needed by patrons who cannot easily visit the building. By any of these methods the librarian is asked a question by the patron and the librarian responds with the best possible answer based on what sources are the most reliable. Some questions can be answered immediately, some require research, and some may require a referral to another library or other institution. This is a service that libraries have provided since the late nineteenth century. Patrons are not expected to know what is in most reference books, so librarians who are knowledgeable about their collection are able to search more easily and find the information requested. Librarians learn to engage patrons in an interview to determine exactly what the patron wants. Sometimes this is immediately obvious, and sometimes it takes some carefully worded follow-up questions to clarify the question being asked. Patrons are often shy about asking their question, so their first attempt does not always convey exactly what their information need is.

The wider variety of options as to how to contact a librarian with a question has been made much easier for those who cannot easily visit a library. Depending on how quickly the information is needed, the format of the information as requested by the patron, and what method of reference service is most comfortable, the patron has several choices. Due to the amount of digitized information available, the user can often get a great deal of full text even if they cannot visit a library. Both email and chat offer more extensive possibilities, but telephone reference is still available for those more comfortable with that method. Reference service continues to be an important part of services to adults.

Readers' advisory services has become a very popular part of adult services. Patrons like to receive recommended reading suggestions. There are now several databases such as *Novelist* and *What Should I Read Next?* that can be used to locate titles that may be of interest to the patron. Other websites of interest are goodreads.com and librarything.com. Although face-to-face interviews can be the most successful, requests for reading suggestions by telephone, email, and chat can also be quite satisfactory. Libraries provide both active and passive readers' advisory services. Active readers' advisory includes one-to-one advice, book talks, author visits, and book discussions. Passive readers' advisory includes providing displays of suggested reading and providing short annotated lists of those titles in the library or on the library's website. For those who don't want something specific, this is often a useful way to find some possible next reads. Some libraries provide a great deal of readers' advisory services on their websites. Examples are the Morton Grove (Illinois) Public Library and the New York Public Library. Readers' advisory was once confined to fiction, but it has expanded to nonfiction and even to audiovisual materials.

Although it has had previous names, such as guidance and orientation to the library, as part of adult services, today it is called information literacy. We define information literacy as providing information to individuals and groups about the library so they will be better equipped to do their research projects. This may be a one-on-one conversation or it may be a group presentation. It is important that people know how to use the library in order to get started on their quest for information or to do research. Users may still need to consult a librarian, but information literacy gives them a chance to work on their own as well.

Collections

Collections for adults began as book collections. Library collections are developed to meet recreational and educational needs. As new formats have developed, public libraries acquired them. Public libraries acquired magazines, large print books, audiovisual materials, digital materials such as e-books and databases, and much more. Public libraries try to acquire a wide variety of materials in each format to satisfy the needs and interests of their users. They follow the ALA Library Bill of Rights, which says that "libraries should provide materials and information presenting all points of view" (American Library Association 2019). Everyone will not like or want to read all the materials a library selects, but it is important that the library have a wide range of materials so that it can meet many points of view and many interests. (See chapter 10 on collections, which discusses collection development statement/policies and how libraries select materials for their collections.)

Programming

Programming is now a large part of adult services. Public libraries provide a wide variety of programming, some aimed at a particular part of the adult population and others of more general interest. Among the programs popular with adults are book discussion groups; book/film discussions; poetry readings and slams; author presentations; cultural performances, which are often provided by local residents; programs about jobs and careers, such as résumé-writing and interview techniques; and classes, which can range from subject-based classes taught by university professors and writing workshops to more active classes such as yoga or exercise classes. More recently libraries have begun to plan and sponsor discussions on topics of current interest. Often programs lead library patrons to books to read on the subject as well as films to view. Programs should be geared to the interests of the community.

Current Information Programming

Many libraries are providing programs on current issues both of local interest and of more regional, national, or global interest. Libraries have found that people want information on many issues, and the library provides a neutral place for information and discussion. The Sno-Isle Libraries inaugurated in 2010 "Issues That Matter" forums. Each forum is developed into a program using local experts and local agencies. The forums are repeated in several libraries in the two counties in Washington state served by the library system. Some of the topics covered have included income tax, legalization of recreational marijuana, same-sex marriage, drugs, bullying, hate crimes, homelessness, and mental health. A panel of local experts presents the program for the evening. The library provides both information and additional resources, including books and other education materials and links to local agencies. It was discovered early on that the audience wanted more than information; they also wanted some action items, so that is included in the programming. Many useful partnerships for the library have developed out of these forums (Pratt, Gustafson, and Batdorf 2019).

At the Skokie (Illinois) Public Library, the staff has developed Civic Lab Pop-Ups, which provide information and resources about issues affecting the community. Each Civic Lab Pop-Up has a specific topic, supporting resources and conversation starters, activities, a resource handout, and direct staff facilitation. There is at least one pop-up each month, and they are offered twice. Topics fall into four categories: topics in the news, such as immigration; basic civic literacy, such as how a bill becomes a law; timely topics, such as taxes in March; and news literacy, such as "What Is Journalism? (And What Isn't)." The Skokie staff continues to develop this approach to programming (Koester 2019).

The Sacramento Public Library (California) has developed a series called "Let's Talk" using local organizations and individuals to provide the information. Recent topics have included health literacy, civility, and climate change.

Arts and Crafts Programming

Arts and crafts programming attracts a large number of local library users. It can be lectures on an exhibit in a local museum, craft workshops on new crafts to try, or a knitting group that meets weekly. This programming provides a way for many local users to meet and talk as well as attend a program. Cultural programming also fits into this category, such as introducing the users to a new group of immigrants and their arts and crafts, which might be embroidery, paper flower craft, or crocheting.

Figure 9.1. A group of library users are crafting fidget blankets in the Makerspace room at the Ames Free Public Library. *Ames Free Library of Easton, Massachusetts.*

Career and Job Programming

On a continuing basis there are many in need of assistance with finding a job and all the work that goes into being prepared for the job search, such as learning how to do a job search, taking computer classes and learning new computer programs, writing a résumé, and practicing the job interview. As an example of expressing what many are thinking, one library ran a program on "What to Do When You Can't Do What You Used to Do." Some of this assistance can be one to one, but sometimes people feel more comfortable at a group program. Although there are many other sources of assistance, the library is one of the few places where all the assistance is free. This is also a good place for partnerships since there are other community organizations that offer career and job preparation that would want to join forces with the library.

Computer Training

Computer training remains a popular programming area for libraries. There are still people who need the basics, while others are interested in learning new computer programs that are more specialized or learning to code. Most computer classes have a fee attached, while the library provides classes free of charge. Free classes are needed since many cannot afford to pay the fees for classes and also may want to learn about a particular program, not knowing whether it will in fact be useful to them.

Figure 9.2.   Library users often gather to discuss books of interest. *Kali9/(E+) via Getty Images.*

Health Programming

Libraries have been on the forefront of developing consumer health information and programs for their users. First is the need to find out about health literacy in the community that the library serves and what resources may be needed. Second, the library should be gathering health literacy resources on local health issues at different reading levels and information in other languages as well as English. Third is the need for general programs on how to maintain good health and those more specific programs, such as what a vegetarian or vegan diet is, basic information on exercise, yoga classes, and presentations on handling blood pressure or diabetes or other diseases common in the community. Many ideas are available through the Public Library Association and its partner, the National Network of Libraries of Medicine (NNLM). The Public Library Association has a website: Healthy Community Tools for Public Libraries (http://publiclibrary.health). NNLM offers informational webinars and classes for librarians about health programming. Public libraries can identify local partners that are also interested in community health such as public health departments and hospitals; local chapters of national health organizations such as the American Heart Association will want to participate in library programs and in health information sharing.

Programs for adults might be organized as a series for the community or for one particular part of the community, such as immigrants who are taking English for speakers of other languages (ESOL), older adults, new mothers, or people dealing with a particular health issue. In addition to being aware of community health information needs, it is important to be aware of what is called "cultural humility," which means understanding the cultural differences in the population the library is serving. Not all cultures have the same attitude toward health, so it is important to understand these differences (Andrews, Kim, and Watanabe 2018).

Services to Groups

Often it is useful to develop services or programs to serve particular groups within the adult community. While all adult users are welcome to take advantage of these services and programs, the library particularly wants to meet the needs of a specific group of adults. In general, services and programs to groups of adults include providing collections and resources of interest to that group, providing services especially of interest and use to that group,

Figure 9.3. Many public libraries offer craft programs for their users. *Courtesy of the Wallingford Public Library, Connecticut.*

and providing programs of interest to that group. The groups that a library chooses to focus on will probably differ from community to community. Some examples of these groups are immigrants, teachers, older adults, people looking for jobs, and the newly retired. Sometimes surveys and focus groups are useful to identify these groups or, one could say, areas of interest.

Serving Emerging Adults

An article by Oleg Kagan (2019) in *Public Libraries* discussed the need for public libraries to support emerging adults. This article, which defined *emerging adults* as from nineteen to thirty years of age, discussed the need for these emerging adults to get assistance in defining what they might want to do. If adults in this age range don't attend college, they often don't receive the kind of advice or mentoring that would help them plan for their future. Libraries can develop partnerships with local groups and especially with community colleges that might be able to offer mentoring to this group. Library programming on writing résumés, going for interviews, and so forth, and accompanying collections can also help bridge this gap.

Services to the Adults Experiencing Homelessness and At-Risk Adults

Public libraries encounter many people experiencing homelessness in their buildings. Homeless shelters are often closed during the day, so the homeless must find another place to spend the day. Many choose to spend their day in libraries. As a result, libraries have developed ways to provide needed services to this part of their user population that are both creative and respectful. For libraries it is important to provide some kind of training for staff members to make them more aware of issues involved with their homeless population. Libraries should examine their policies and procedures so they are treating the homeless in the same way as they would treat any patron. The ALA Public Library Association has a Social Worker Task Force that has published "Public Library: Overview of Trauma-Informed Care." These guidelines encourage separating behavior issues from the person themselves and not labeling people who may be homeless or have some other trauma issue. They encourage creating welcoming spaces for all users.

One model is that of the Dallas Public Library in Texas. The library has set up a "Coffee and Conversation" program so the homeless feel welcome in the library and can have a conversation with the staff of the library. The staff wants to know how they can better serve this part of their user population. There is a HELP (Homeless Engagement and Leadership Program) Desk at the Dallas Public Library where the homeless can get information on any issue of concern to them. The library also provides access to the internet for the homeless as well as other library patrons.

Partnerships are a very useful way for public libraries to serve the homeless. At the San José (California) Public Library, the "Social Workers in the Library" program was developed in partnership with the San José State University School of Social Work and the National Association of Social Workers. Twenty-minute appointments are offered for anyone who has a problem.

But because of the large homeless population in San José, many who sign up for the appointments are homeless. There are many organizations that work nationwide with the homeless and are possible partners for libraries, such as the Salvation Army, Catholic Charities USA, and local homeless shelters. Libraries can offer a variety of classes for the homeless, including help for job seekers, computer instruction, story times for children, literacy classes, and, of course, books to borrow.

The Salt Lake City Public Library partnered with the Salt Lake City government and Volunteers of America to organize and host Project Uplift, a resource fair for at-risk individuals that brought together more than thirty community organizations, businesses, and service providers tackling homelessness.

In rural Iowa the libraries have partnered with local groups that serve the homeless. In Marion, Iowa, the library serves as a warming station and as a heat-relief site. The Marion Library has led a group of local organizations that are trying to provide a safety net for those on the verge of becoming homeless. In Cedar Rapids, the Willis Dady Homeless Services holds weekly office hours in the library.

Many public libraries have added social workers to their staff as well as peer navigators, who are people who have once been homeless. The social workers are available to identify and communicate with patrons who are dealing with a variety of issues from homelessness to mental health issues, hunger, and drug abuse. These social workers often provide some basic training to the library staff on dealing with patrons who are homeless or have other related issues. They work on relationship building and on using community resources to assist those in need.

Services to Ethnic Groups

Services to four major groups—African Americans, Hispanics, Asian Americans, and Native Americans—can provide a template for working with ethnic groups in the United States.

African Americans lacked access to libraries and were only allowed to have their own library branches in the twentieth century. The *Plessy v. Ferguson* decision by the Supreme Court in 1896 legalized separate libraries for African Americans, and the decision held until *Brown v. Board of Education* in 1954. Integration came slowly. Many large city library systems made efforts to reach out to African Americans to provide them with library cards, offer appropriate library materials by and about African Americans, hire African American staff, plan programs of interest, and reach out into their communities. In 1970, the Black Caucus of ALA was formed and is now an affiliate of ALA. This organization promotes the development of library services and collections for African Americans.

Hispanics from many countries have been in the United States for decades, but outreach by public libraries has been slow. The language barrier kept many from communicating effectively, and buying collections of books in Spanish of interest to their Hispanic users lagged. Slowly, Spanish language collections have become more available. Libraries who have large Hispanic populations have tried to hire bilingual staff to better communicate with their Hispanic users. ALA/RUSA has developed "Guidelines for Library Services for Spanish-Speaking Library Users," approved in 2007 to assist libraries to provide extended services. The guidelines cover collections, programs, services and community relations, personnel, and facilities. REFORMA is an ALA affiliate that has been active in providing information and support to libraries developing services to their Hispanic community.

Libraries have developed services for Asian Americans. Collections and bilingual staff were added to better communicate with the Asian American communities, which were for many decades overwhelmingly Chinese. Some large cities developed branches mostly serving the Chinese and other Asian Americans. These included the Los Angeles Public Library, the San Francisco Public Library, Chicago Public Library, and the New York Public Library. The APALA (Asian Pacific American Library Association), an affiliate of the American Library Association, provides support to libraries servicing Asian American communities, as does the Chinese American Librarians Association, also an affiliate of ALA.

Native Americans are the fourth group. Libraries, especially on reservations, still struggle to serve this population due to lack of funding. The IMLS (Institute of Museum and Library Services) sponsors funding for library service to Native Americans that has provided needed resources and staff. The American Indian Library Association (AILA), formed in 1979, an affiliate of the American Library Association, supports the work of Native American libraries.

Figure 9.4.   Computers are very important for the library's users, both for finding information and looking for jobs. *Hill Street Studios (Digital Vision).*

Services to Immigrants

Public libraries have a long history of supporting immigrants. In the early part of the twentieth century, immigrants came to public libraries to read and learn, and they still do today. There are many needs that immigrants have that libraries can meet, including learning English, how to become a citizen, information on finding a job, information on the U.S. education system for children and adults, and information on the U.S. health-care system. Other library services for immigrants include welcome signs in the languages of local residents, staff members who are respectful of cultural customs, multilingual staff, English conversation classes, small business information, financial literacy classes, and digital literacy classes.

One of the most experienced public libraries in serving immigrants is the Queens Public Library. Their New Americans program has been serving immigrants for many decades. The library provides English as second language classes; preparation for citizenship classes; legal assistance; programs on immigration law, tenants' rights, career planning, starting a business, education, and health; and a variety of cultural programs in the languages of the people in each branch's neighborhood. Books are provided in more than thirty-two languages. The library's website lists each language and which branches have books in that language.

The American Library Association's Public Programs Office has published a white paper, *New American Library Project*, on how libraries are serving immigrants. The white paper provides information on what libraries are doing and recommendations for programming. Of particular interest is the discussion of libraries working with local organizations to provide services for immigrants. This can be as basic as providing space for an organization's classes or programs or cooperatively planning a project for the community's immigrants. Public libraries have many opportunities to serve their immigrant population, especially offering programs that do not depend heavily on English, such as cooking and craft classes.

Other libraries have served a need for naturalization ceremonies. The public libraries of Hillsboro, Oregon, and Memphis, Tennessee, are examples of libraries that have hosted naturalization ceremonies. Working with the U.S. Citizenship and Immigration Services (USCIS), they meet the requirement for a neutral space and plan the naturalization ceremony following the requirements of the USCIS. By doing this, they introduce new American citizens and their families to the library and its many resources and encourage them to get library cards and use the library (Osuna and Reich 2019).

Services to Older Adults

Older adults have always been users of public libraries. The number of adults over sixty-five years of age continues to grow, and, by 2050, it is estimated that 19 percent of the U.S. population will be over the age of sixty-five. Public libraries have always served older adults, but now more than ever services and programs are needed. Not only are there many older adults, but there are also many active older adults looking for more substantive library resources and more programs and services. The latest "Guidelines for Library Services with 60+ Audience: Best Practices," published by the American Library Association's Reference and User Services Association in 2017, addresses some of the ways libraries can serve older adults. Staff can use some training in order to provide the best services to this audience. The guidelines suggest asking a local organization with expertise in this area to design and provide staff training. It is recommended that public libraries designate someone to be in charge of serving older adults as one of their responsibilities.

Libraries should provide facilities that accommodate users with accessibility issues. This could include meeting ADA guidelines, as well as providing good levels of lighting, spaces between shelving that can accommodate walkers and wheelchairs, chairs in places where older adults might want to sit down, assistive technology for vision and hearing issues, and adaptive hardware and information on programs and services in fourteen-point type.

Collections are an important part of what this older adult population wants. In addition to the usual new books and other materials on all subjects, the library should acquire materials on issues of special interest to older adults, such as finance, travel for older adults, making decisions about future housing, and health. When possible, copies of books in large print should be acquired as well as audiobooks and e-books. Those eligible should be introduced to the Library for the Blind and Physically Handicapped program, which is part of the Library of Congress with regional branches throughout the United States that provide free books and other reading matter to those with vision problems.

Although many of the library's programs will be of interest to older adults, some special programming will be welcomed. Technology training is very popular for this group that came of age before the internet. Libraries could provide presentations that promote lifelong learning on financial planning and consumer health, as well as book discussion groups, intergenerational talks, films, craft and ESOL classes, and programs for caregivers, in addition to partnerships with local organizations that serve older adults. Organizations the public library might consider as partners for programs and services include county and town departments on the aging, nursing homes, senior centers, AARP, and local hospitals.

Many public libraries also offer services for older adults who cannot visit the library. This includes delivery to homebound adults and serving institutions such as nursing homes, assisted-living facilities, adult day care, senior centers, and retirement communities.

Services to Veterans

Veterans are an important group in any community and one that can be well served by the public library. This can start with providing information on the library's website, which could include information on veterans' benefits, health care, education, employment, and other areas of interest to veterans.

This is an area where partnerships with organizations serving veterans, such as the local VFW and American Legion posts and state and county offices for veteran services, are useful.

In California a grant enabled the development of thirty-five Veterans Resource Centers in public libraries. Contra Costa Public Library developed an exhibit of images and stories of veterans' tattoos. Los Angeles Public Library worked in cooperation with the Weingardt Center for the Homeless to establish ten veterans' resource centers in their branches staffed by veterans.

There are opportunities for public libraries to hold programs on issues related to veterans, which might include holding book discussions and writing workshops, developing exhibits, doing audio or video recordings of the memories of veterans, and working in partnership with other local organizations to celebrate veterans' holidays. Other libraries use holidays such as Veterans Day as a time to acknowledge their local veterans. If there is a veterans' home in the area, libraries can provide materials and programs. Programs featuring films about war with a discussion following it is a good way to draw in veterans. Veterans have many stories about their experiences, and teens will especially be interested in finding out about these experiences.

The Library of Congress has been running the Veterans History Project since 2000. Many libraries have interviewed and recorded the memories of U.S. veterans in their communities, and these interviews are now kept at the Library of Congress. Libraries can provide a wide variety of services for veterans.

Services to the LGBTQ Community

Libraries have served their LGBTQ (lesbian, gay, bisexual, transgender, and queer/questioning) community through their resource collections, but not always through programming and exhibits. Many factors have stood in the way, including local community acceptance. But much has changed, and libraries are now providing positive and often excellent services to their LGBTQ community, which includes children, teens, and adults. The first thing to consider is the library's collection. Strong collections for all ages are a must. Libraries can promote this collection with booklists of recommended readings. Programming is another way to show that the library wants to serve this community. This includes visits by LGBTQ authors to discuss their work, and films on LGBTQ subjects can provide appropriate programming. There are more mainstream films now available as well as many independent films. The history of the LGBTQ community can often be captured in library exhibits. Groups such as PFLAG (Parents, Families and Friends of Lesbian and Gays) are also ready to help with library programming. Libraries should be particularly aware of gay teens who need to feel accepted in a world that provides mixed messages, so good collections and programming will be of interest to them.

Services to the Business Community

Libraries can provide many services to both existing local businesses and people wanting to start a business. For those trying to start a business, libraries often provide basic information on the legal steps of forming a business, space for meetings with clients, and programs on various aspects of running a business, such as finances and marketing. Libraries also supply computers, computer supplies, fax machines, printers, and so forth. For existing businesses, libraries often host meetings of business people where they can hear a speaker and network with other business people. Sometimes businesses need assistance with marketing through social media or perhaps understanding new laws pertaining to businesses.

Services to People with Disabilities

Public libraries serve many people with disabilities, which can be physical, developmental, or intellectual. Libraries have now developed many new programs and services to meet the needs of people of all ages with disabilities. For those struggling with print books, there are also large print books, audiobooks, and even Braille. This is a group eager to use libraries. Public libraries have worked to make their buildings handicapped accessible and to provide services and programs. As an example of these services, the Sacramento Public Library (California) developed Access ABILITY to reach out to users with disabilities and their families. Several branches are part of this project, with staff members trained to provide appropriate services and programs for this population. Sacramento gives priority to hiring staff with disabilities working in these branches. Other public libraries offer book clubs for people with disabilities.

Services to Rural Areas

In a rural library the first thing is to get to know the community and what the community needs. Many have never thought about what resources the library can bring to the community. Libraries can show how they can contribute to the community through its resources, available space for programming, and working with local organizations to support their work. Libraries can share their space with local groups that do not have the financial ability to have their own location. Mobile library service is often available for those too far to make regular trips to the library.

New and Interesting Services

Libraries continue to explore new programs and services that will be of interest to their patrons. At the Free Library of Philadelphia there is now a kitchen where patrons learn about reading recipes and how to measure ingredients. This has also been folded into the ESOL programs for those learning English. At the District of Columbia Public Library, the new main building will have a floor dedicated to nonprofits. The Queens Public Library follows up with prisoners they have worked with and has a branch where the prisoners can go once released, helping them get started with the job search.

In conclusion, public libraries have many and varied opportunities to serve the adult population in their community. Both new and more traditional resources and services are usually of interest to the library's clientele. Everyone still wants a list of good books to read—both new ones and ones they might have missed. Some users will still want print books, and others will want the digital version; therefore, public libraries must be prepared to serve both ends of the spectrum. Users of public libraries are also grateful to have a quiet place to sit and read or to be able to reserve and pick up a new book quickly. Not everyone will use the library in the same way. Programs can bring together people of like interests who might not have met each other in the course of their daily life. Many programs, even for specific groups, are of interest to others. Adult services is an important component of public library service, ready to listen and respond to community needs, whether in person or remotely.

Discussion Questions

1. What groups do you think will be the easiest to reach with library services?

2. What programs will reach a variety of audiences?

Bibliography

Albright, Meagan. 2006. The Public Library's Responsibilities to LGBT Communities. *Public Libraries* 45 (5): 52–56.

American Library Association. 2019. "Library Bill of Rights." Accessed December 14, 2020. http://www.ala.org/advocacy/intfreedom/librarybill.

Andrews, Nicola, Sunny Kim, and Josie Watanabe. 2018. "Cultural Humility as a Transformative Framework for Librarians, Tutors, and Youth Volunteers: Applying a Lens of Cultural Responsiveness in Training Library Staff and Volunteers." *Young Adult Library Services* 16, no. 2 (Winter): 19–22.

Jarvis, Madeline. 2019. "Libraries Lead: Homeless Prevention and Advocacy in Rural Iowa." *Public Libraries* 58 (5): 25–28.

Kagan, Oleg. 2019. "Five Things Libraries Need to Know about Emerging Adults." *Public Libraries* 58, no. 4 (July/August): 11–13.

Koerber, Jennifer. 2016. "Celebrate and Integration." *Library Journal* 141 (10): 48–51.

Koester, Amy. 2019. "A Civic Initiative about Information: The Civic Lab at Skokie Public Library." *Public Libraries* 58, no. 4 (July/August): 45–52.

Nichols, Joel A. 2016. "Serving All Library Families in a Queer and Gender Queer Way." *Public Libraries* 55, no. 1 (January/February). http://publiclibrariesonline.org.

Osuna, Linda, and Carol Reich. 2019. "Welcome to the United States: Naturalization Ceremonies at Your Public Library." *Public Libraries* 58, no. 4 (July/August): 54–59.

Perry, Claudia A. (2014). "Information Services to Older Adults: Initial Findings from a Survey of Suburban Libraries." *Library Quarterly* 84, no. 3 (July): 348–86.

Pratt, Charles, Sonia Gustafson, and Kurt Batdorf. 2019. "Issues That Matter: Forums Build Civic Engagement." *Public Libraries* 58, no. 4 (July/August): 35–43.

Reference and User Services Association (RUSA). 2017. "Guidelines for Library Service with 60+ Audience: Best Practices." www.ala.org/rusa.

———. n.d. "Our History." Accessed December 11, 2020. www.ala.org/rusa/our-history.

Roy, Loriene. 2000. "To Support and Model Native American Library Service." *Texas Library Journal* 75, no. 1 (Spring): 32–35.

Roy, Loriene, Marin Barker, Lanita L. Hidalgo, and Frances A. Rickard. 2016. "Public Library Services for Veterans: Selected Brief Case Studies." *Public Library Quarterly* 35 (3): 222–42.

Shaw, Lisa M. 2019. "The Maine Point." *Public Libraries* 58 (5): 23–25.

Stephens, Annabel. 2006. "Twenty-First Century Public Library Adult Services." *RUSA Quarterly* 45, no. 3 (Spring): 223–35.

Vincent, John. 2015. "Why Do We Need to Bother? Public Library Services to LGBTQ People." *Library Trends* 64, no. 2 (Fall): 285–98.

COLLECTIONS AND COLLECTION DEVELOPMENT

- Overview and definitions
- Selection and selection tools
- Organization of selection
- Collection development policies/statements
- Developing and managing the materials budget
- Formats collected
- Acquisitions
- Vendors and licensing
- Gifts
- Weeding
- Replacements
- Storage and preservation
- Inventories
- Collection analysis
- Intellectual freedom
- Outline of a collection development policy/statement

Overview and Definitions

Public library collections offer books, audiovisual materials, e-resources, and other formats that are the heart of a public library. They are acquired to meet the needs of their community of patrons. Public libraries provide access to the latest titles that will be of interest to its community. Some public libraries have archival collections, especially about their community—that is, local history—but this is usually not the main focus of the library's collection. The public library serves as a place for information, education, and recreation. It is also a gathering place for the community to meet and discuss the issues of the day. Library collections provide the best sellers, the classics, and much more. They are a place in the community where many voices and many points of view can be found. Anyone in a community can have a library card and borrow books, and many other formats of materials are available. Materials that are not available on-site can usually be obtained through interlibrary loan.

In the beginning in the United States, there were social libraries and subscription libraries where people could both read and discuss in the library or borrow books. Many who had no other way to get a formal education came to the library to read and learn. Early libraries required some payment in order to be a member, but starting with the Peterborough (New Hampshire) Town Library in 1833, the number of free public libraries began to grow, with the Boston Public Library being the first free public library in a large city. Andrew Carnegie expanded greatly the number of public libraries in the United States by providing funding for small towns and large cities to build libraries, as long as the local government agreed to provide continued funding for them.

Public libraries add materials to their collections year round. *Collection development* is defined as the process of selecting new materials for the library collection. This includes identifying library needs, finding reviews, and then acquiring the materials through an appropriate vendor. If these resources are electronic, the library may have to develop contracts with the vendors. Collection management involves the work with collections once the materials are acquired, which includes managing the materials budget, weeding, evaluation of the collection, storage, and preservation. Collection management also includes marketing the collection.

Selection and Selection Tools

Selection in public libraries requires a great deal of knowledge and skill. Even in the early part of the twentieth century library selection was based on selecting the best quality books, sometimes called "good" books. This meant that some very popular titles were never or seldom purchased. Starting in the 1960s, this philosophy began to change as libraries made more effort to buy popular titles that the public wanted, even if they did not qualify as "good literature." Today, libraries collect a wide variety of titles to meet the needs and interests of their community.

There are a number of ways to identify resources to consider for the collection. These include reading review sources such as *Kirkus Reviews*, *Publishers Weekly*, *Library Journal*, *School Library Journal*, and *Booklist*. Other materials are identified through publishers' catalogs, bookstores and book fairs, library conference exhibits, and user requests.

The criteria used for purchase decisions include

- subject,

- accuracy,

- writing style,

- currency,

- authoritativeness of author and publisher,

- appropriate reading level for intended patrons,

- treatment of the subject, and

- cost.

Public library selectors try to acquire materials that will be of interest to their community. Public library collections are not research collections but rather current, living collections responding to contemporary needs and interests. Public librarians depend on interlibrary loan for books not in demand but requested by a user. If a number of patrons request a book or other material, the library usually decides to buy it if they can afford it. Many public libraries do a great deal of title-by-title selection in order to ensure that the funds spent are truly titles that will be of interest. Public librarians often buy more than one copy of a book or other resource and in more than one format if it is in high demand. For example, fiction may be purchased in print (hardcover and paperback), as an e-book, as an audiobook, and in large print. The number purchased will depend on the amount of the collections budget that can be allocated for this purpose. Librarians selecting materials also try to balance the collections to allow for several points of view.

Selection tools often cover all types of formats, while others are more specialized. Librarians often use *Kirkus Reviews* and *Publishers Weekly* for pre-publication ordering. They review print and e-book materials that are of interest to the general public. *Library Journal, School Library Journal,* and *Booklist* review print materials and a selection of audiovisual materials and e-resources as close to publication date as possible. *Library Journal* reviews materials for all ages and most formats. *School Library Journal* reviews materials for children and young adults in many formats. *Booklist* reviews print, audiovisual materials, and e-resources for all ages. Since it is sometimes difficult to predict the demand for a book, public libraries often use rental collections to meet user needs. One example of this is the McNaughton Lease plan from Brodart Books & Library Services, where libraries receive multiple copies of adult or young adult books in demand and can return them when the demand has slowed down. A rental fee is charged by the vendor for this service. Audio and video titles are harder to identify, but some useful review sources for public libraries are *Library Journal, School Library Journal, Booklist,* and *Billboard*.

Organization of Selection

Public librarians usually select titles individually for their collections rather than taking advantage of materials packages. This is because materials budgets are often small and every dollar counts. Selection can be organized in a variety of ways. One common way to organize is assigning the staff members, usually librarians, certain subject areas (e.g., biographies) or formats (e.g., audio material) and having them select appropriate materials within the budget they have been allocated. Or there may be staff committees charged with the responsibility of selecting materials. The responsibility is twofold: selecting materials to meet community needs and staying within the budget. Now, in larger public libraries, title-by-title ordering has become too time consuming since librarians are needed to provide information services, plan programs, and provide other library services. In larger public libraries there is usually a selection committee that selects titles for all the units in the system. This does not mean that title-by-title selection at a branch or departmental level no longer exists. Most systems make some individual selection possible to allow for the specific interests of the patrons. Many techniques are used to ensure that a central selection committee has enough information to make appropriate choices. This could be by periodic surveys of the units and/or branches or by visiting the units and/or branches periodically to see if they are receiving the materials they need.

The advantage of centralized selection is that selection can be made more quickly and ordered from the vendor so that best sellers and other books of great interest to the community can be acquired before the actual publication date. Vendors have placed their holdings online so that libraries can efficiently select titles and order them in advance of publication date. This both benefits the library and its patrons and is also very cost-effective. Title-by-title selection by units or branches is often a little slower but can also be effective. Each title is chosen by reading the online reviews. There is perhaps less waste of dollars this way since the books and other formats are chosen with a particular user population in mind. But it is more labor intensive and thus more expensive in the use of staff time. Many librarians will argue that title-by-title selection is an important part of their work, while others find that centralized selection is satisfactory.

Collection Development Policies/Statements

Although some would argue that collection development policies or statements are too time consuming to write and to keep up to date, many others argue that a library without a collection development policy is a library without a plan. If all the librarians involved in selection are on their own, it can result in too much of one type of resource and not enough of another. The balance can be thrown off by the lack of upfront planning; therefore, most libraries choose to have a collection development plan/statement. Some are more detailed than others, and that is the prerogative of the library. Collection development/statements should be updated on a regular basis.

Some of the benefits of a collection development plan or policy are the following:

1. Provides a consistent plan for all staff members who are involved in selection. Selection staff may have a tendency to buy books they want to read, so it is good to have an overall plan for them to follow. Many libraries provide some overall guidelines, subject by

subject, indicating what level of material is needed and what the demand is in a particular subject area. For example, there may be a large demand for books on health but less demand for philosophy books. It may also indicate how the library sees trends, such as in the area of e-books and other e-resources and streaming audio and video, and how it plans to move forward in these areas.

2. Sets institutional priorities and selection criteria for collection development. It is important to inform everyone as to what the library's priorities are and what criteria it uses in selecting materials. This is useful to both the staff and the public. It also gives the library a way to respond to questions from patrons about individual purchases.

3. Provides a plan for acquiring electronic resources, a plan that can be different from print resources. The decisions libraries make about electronic resources such as databases can be different from those they make about other materials. Electronic resources are usually more expensive, often come in packages of resources, and require more long-term commitment. So decisions made about them need to be recorded for future selectors.

4. Provides information on the strengths and weaknesses of the collection. It is important to be aware of the strengths and weaknesses of the various parts of the library collection and whether they are purposeful or just in need of being developed. The subject-by-subject guidelines can be quite useful for understanding selection goals. Audiovisual materials should also be included since there is a need here too to indicate the goals of selection in this area.

5. Provides information to new staff on how the library views collection development. New staff members charged with doing selection need guidelines to follow. They need to know the level of acquisitions required in a certain subject area. The collection development policy/statement is a way to accomplish this.

6. Provides guidance on how the materials budget will be spent. By identifying the priorities of the library's collection, there will be guidance as to how the materials budget will be spent. No library

can buy everything, so it is important to understand the priorities. It is important to provide information about how decisions about popular titles and multiple copies of titles will be made.

7. Provides information for library patrons on how the library selects its resources. Both the collection priorities and the selection criteria help to inform as to how the library will spend its materials budget. It is important to identify subject areas that will not be purchased or will be seldom purchased versus subject areas where great depth of resources is needed.

8. Guides staff as to how to handle complaints and protects the library against outside pressures. The guidelines in the policy/statement as to how the library handles complaints about materials in the collection will help the staff and the user to follow correct procedures. Libraries usually have a form to fill out for the member of the public who has a complaint about a book or other resource in the collection. This is the first step in dealing with the complaint. There will be other steps leading to a decision by the board of trustees that will be conveyed to the member of the public.

9. Provides a public relations document. The collection development policy/statement should be on the library's website and otherwise available to the public.

Developing and Managing the Materials Budget

Materials budgets can be handled in many ways. Once the budget is set for the year, the library may want to break down the materials budget into smaller budget categories in order to keep track of the spending in each part of the materials budget; for example, children's books, young adult books, adult books, magazines and newspapers, audio materials, video materials, and special dedicated funds. These are often called allocations.

Materials budgets are developed based on the expenditures in the last fiscal year plus projected increases in the cost of library materials. There are many ways to find information on predicted price increases for the next year. The annual *Library and Book Trade Almanac* provides information on materials prices. Also, *Library Journal* does an annual Periodicals Price Survey.

Figure 10.1. Libraries offer things other than books to their users. At Ames Free Public Library, they offer users a chance to borrow and use a telescope. *Ames Free Library of Easton, Massachusetts.*

Publishers Weekly provides information on materials prices, and *School Library Journal* publishes an annual list of average book prices. Finally, some vendors publish information on pricing for the coming year. Most libraries monitor the materials budget on a monthly basis to be sure they are on target for their expenditures. This should take into account that publishing has its own highs and lows. There are two main publishing seasons: the larger one is in the fall and a slightly smaller one in the spring. The staff doing selection should take the publishing seasons into account when deciding how the money will be spent.

Many libraries divide their budget by percentages per month so they can better evaluate if they are spending at the appropriate level. This is usually not the same percentage each month, not only because of the publishing seasons but also because libraries want to have all their materials on order in advance of the end of the budget year. Public libraries will want to run either a cash budget for materials expenditures or an accrual budget. If they have a cash budget, then the expenditures will be recorded when the bills for materials purchased come into the library. This allows the library to know exactly how much it has spent. But it does not allow for orders that have not yet arrived. If the library decides to have an accrual budget, then the amount of each purchase will be subtracted from the materials budget when the order is placed. This means that the expenditure is only an estimate since the discount may not be what the library expected. Sometimes materials ordered do not arrive during the fiscal year, so the library may want to cancel these orders before the end of the fiscal year and use the funds for some other orders. In many libraries the funds for the collections budget cannot be carried over to the next year; therefore, it is important to monitor the budget and to have a plan for spending out the budget. For example, e-materials can be ordered and received very quickly.

Small public library budgets are the hardest to handle. They may not have enough funds to buy all the formats patrons want, so careful selection is needed. They may have patrons who want to read in other languages, which may be difficult for the library to include in its budget. Finally, they

Figure 10.2. Libraries provide accessibility for all users. *simonkr/(E+) via Getty Images.*

may need multiple copies of titles, which is not affordable with their budget. Sometimes groups such as the Friends of the Library can raise additional money for the materials budget.

Formats Collected

Public libraries have been the most open to acquiring new formats. They have also been willing to change as needed since not all formats have remained popular and others have replaced them especially in the audiovisual area. Sometimes libraries keep an older format for a time if their patrons still have the equipment for it.

Print books were for many decades the staple of public libraries, and even today they remain the most popular part of the library's collection. Books have developed from the original hardcover print to paperbacks, large print books, e-books, and audiobooks, although in other types of libraries, such as academic libraries, fewer print books are purchased when e-books are available. In public libraries e-books are just one of the choices for the library patron, and not all library patrons prefer e-books. Many patrons read both print books and e-books as well as listen to audiobooks. Print includes magazines and newspapers, which have been more popular as e-resources than books.

Figure 10.3. Books provide a way for people to meet and talk. *pixelfit/(E+) via Getty Images.*

Graphic novels, small press books, and self-published books are also popular in public libraries. Graphic novels and graphic nonfiction are available for all ages now and are especially popular with young adults. Sometimes they call for additional review since they are not always appropriate for all audiences. Small press books have slowly gained a larger audience, especially when they exhibit at library conferences. In the past, libraries seldom purchased self-published books. But this has changed, especially because many self-published books are now reviewed by major reviewing sources. Certain categories of self-published books are of particular interest to public libraries, such as local history, travel, history, how-to-do-it books, and books of local interest.

The first e-resources acquired by libraries were newspaper and magazine articles in the form of databases. Books were a later entry into the e-resource collections of public libraries. E-books are very popular with the public, although public libraries have struggled to provide them because of the pricing policies of publishers. Publishers continue to charge exorbitant prices for popular titles or delay the availability of them.

Audiovisual materials have long been part of public library collections. They began with the disks, including 78 rpm and 33 1/3 rpm. The disks were replaced first by cassettes and then by CDs and now by streaming audio. Video began with 16-mm films and then after many iterations to DVDs and streaming videos.

Public libraries often acquire packages of digital materials. Among these packages are Hoopla, which provides e-books, audiobooks, comics, music, movies, and TV shows; RB Digital, which provides magazines, audiobooks, e-books, movies, comics, graphic novels, and TV shows; Overdrive, which provides e-books, audiobooks, video, and music; Kanopy, which provides film; and Freegal, which provides music. This marks a departure from the tradition of title-by-title selection. However, the pricing of these packages makes it most appealing to public libraries, and users can find a wide variety of interesting resources in one place.

Acquisitions

Decisions as to where to send orders to be fulfilled are made in the acquisitions department. Libraries usually work with more than one vendor. There are many reasons for the decisions made, which include discounts, speed of fulfillment, and format of the material sought. Here are some terms used in acquisitions:

Firm orders. Materials are ordered title by title.

Standing orders. Titles for which the library wants each successive volume or title to be sent automatically. This could include a wide range of material from reference annuals to annual travel books.

Approval plans. Programs where the library outlines in advance its collection profile and then the vendor supplies materials that fit those specifications, which could include subject areas, types of material, and price. The vendor can ship the titles selected to the library or provide a list of possible titles for the library to make a final selection.

The steps in the acquisitions process are the following:

1. The order is submitted to the acquisitions department.

2. A vendor is identified for the order.

3. The order is sent to the vendor.

4. The order is received by the library.

5. The order is processed and a fund code is assigned to the order.

6. The vendor is paid.

If the order is for e-resources, the acquisitions process is slightly different:

1. The order is submitted to the acquisitions department.

2. A vendor is identified.

3. Acquisitions checks to see if a contract or license is needed and if the library has a contract or license with the vendor.

4. Acquisitions checks to see if this order should be placed directly or through a consortia to which the library belongs.

5. The order is sent to the appropriate vendor or to the consortia.

6. The order is received by the library.

7. The order is processed and a fund code is assigned to the order.

8. The vendor is paid.

Vendors and Licensing

Vendors may sell more than one product. But some vendors specialize in books and e-books from many publishers as well as audiovisual materials. There are subscription agencies that provide periodicals both in print and online. Other vendors may specialize in audio and video products. Many vendors offer packages. For example, e-books can be ordered individually or in packages. Hoopla offers e-books, audiobooks, comics, and music. Magazines can be ordered individually or as an electronic package, such as RB Digital, which offers more than eighty magazines. Discounts for library materials vary, so libraries need to be sure what the discount will be when they work with a vendor. Often it differs from trade books to scholarly books to reference books. Sometimes the discount is deeper if the library buys a larger percentage of its budget from one vendor. What libraries choose to acquire will depend on their budget. If they need many new titles, the packages may prove more cost-effective, even if there are titles the patrons never use. On the other hand, libraries may choose a title-by-title selection so that they are choosing only titles they think their public will read.

Working with vendors calls for developing business relationships with them. Many vendors assign certain sales persons to specific geographic areas or to specific types of libraries. Learning to work with them will make acquisitions work easier, and it is good to find out what is possible with a certain vendor. For example, a vendor can help the library develop lists of titles in a particular subject area or can catalog and process books at a very inexpensive cost. Libraries should never be afraid to ask for something special since it is often something that can easily be accommodated.

Licensing of e-resources is a whole new area for public libraries. When possible, it is best to join a consortium so that the costs will be lower and the library can acquire more of a variety of titles. If the library is acquiring e-resources on its own, it is important to read each contract carefully. First, there is the price consideration. Pricing can be done in a variety of ways, which includes the number of patrons with library cards or the number of branches, pay per use, concurrent patrons, or a flat fee. *Concurrent patrons* mean how many patrons are using the e-resource at any one time. This can be a very small number since very few resources have a large number of patrons using a resource at any one time. Also, there are cases when the vendor will charge an annual flat fee. Some issues to be alert to in contracts are limitations on use (e.g., only by patrons with library cards), the renewal and cancellation process, and laws that will govern any dispute that arises. It should be the state where the library is located, not the state where the company is located.

Gifts

Libraries receive many gift books from their patrons. Gift books are usually older titles that are already in the collection or even books with content that is dated. It is important for the library to have a gift book policy. First of all, the library should say that once the book or other resource is given to the library, it is the property of the library. Second, the library should say that gift books are subject to the same selection criteria as other materials acquired by the library. Third, if the library does not put the book or other resource in the collection, the library should state what might happen to the gift. It could be given to another agency or discarded if dated or in bad condition. Gifts are expensive to handle and even more expensive to catalog and add to the collection, so most libraries are cautious about what they add. Libraries cannot estimate the possible value of a certain title. If the patron thinks the book or other resource is valuable, libraries can offer a list of possible appraisers. For more routine gifts, libraries provide the user with a form to fill out indicating the number of items donated and the possible value. If the patron thinks the value of their gift is more than $250, then a more formal letter can be requested. A sample gift book policy is at the end of the chapter.

Weeding

Weeding or withdrawal of materials is important in public libraries. Many patrons of public libraries are looking for new titles, so libraries must continually weed to make room for new titles. Public library patrons tend not to be researchers, so older titles often just sit on the shelves. The concept of weeding is a hard one for public library patrons to understand. They tend to think that libraries are throwing away "good books" when they weed. There should be guidelines for weeding in the collection development policy/statement. For example, materials may be discarded from the library's collection for the following reasons:

- if the information is out of date,

- if the information is inaccurate,

- if the title was selected in error,

- if newer editions are available,

- if the book or other resource is in poor condition, or

- if the book or other resource is no longer being used by library patrons as indicated by the circulation records.

These guidelines provide the public with information so they have a better idea as to what the considerations are for weeding materials. Weeding can begin with a report from the integrated library system (ILS) about the circulation of material. This can help to quickly identify titles with low circulation. Shelf scanning is also a good method to identify books in poor condition. It is always better to weed slowly and not throw away large quantities of materials at one time. This has caused many libraries huge public relations problems with the public. A few books discarded each month will be less noticeable. Highly recommended is the CREW method, which provides good detailed information on weeding. It is also important to note that some subjects date faster than others. Many libraries develop a chart that indicates when material in a certain subject area needs to be weeded. For example, material in the sciences needs to be weeded more often than art books. Reference books need to be weeded on a regular basis. All formats need to be weeded, not just books.

Replacements

Libraries once replaced many of the books discarded, especially when the book was simply in bad condition. Now there are more possibilities. If the book has had little use in recent years, perhaps the library will not replace it and depend rather on interlibrary loan to fill requests. There is also the possibility of replacing the print book with an e-book. The book is still available and will not wear out so fast. Digital copies save space and are always available when needed.

Storage and Preservation

Storage is another possibility for books not in great demand but that need to be retained. If a library has some storage available, this can be a way to keep some books longer. Reference books are often in this category as well as multiple copies of classics. Criteria for storage include low use, seasonal use, duplicates, and superseded reference volumes.

"Preservation includes selecting replacement copies, moving items to a protected area, and selecting materials for reformatting. Binding, rebinding, repairing, using protective enclosures, controlling use, monitoring environmental conditions, and conserving are preservation activities intended to prolong the useful life of materials" (Johnson 2014, 213). Although public libraries seldom have rare books, some older books that are out of print may need preservation. Most of the time someone on staff can learn how to do some basic preservation work in order to keep these titles in good condition.

Inventories

Many public libraries do inventories to see what books listed in their catalog are no longer available. This is much easier to do now that the information is stored in an online system. Once a list of missing titles is established, the staff can decide if they are candidates for replacements in either print or e-book or whether the title should be removed from the catalog. Having an up-to-date catalog is very important so that patrons are not misled into thinking certain titles are still owned by the library.

Collection Analysis

Collection analysis helps the staff to understand better the use of the collection. Libraries can use both qualitative and quantitative measures to evaluate the collection. Quantitative measures include circulation statistics where the library can see how much a particular title is being used. In-house use statistics can also be reviewed since not all materials circulate. Interlibrary loan statistics show what subject areas might need more material. Qualitative measures include surveys, focus groups, and list checking. These can be used to evaluate whether the collection is strong enough in some subject areas.

Intellectual Freedom

Patrons sometimes challenge or complain about books or other materials in public library collections. Public libraries should be prepared for these challenges. A procedure within the library should be established that any staff member can follow. First of all, there should be a form for the patron to fill out, describing the challenge to material in the library collection. The information on this form will then be evaluated by the librarians involved with selection to decide the next step. The board of trustees will also be informed about the challenge and the next steps recommended. In any case, the user will receive a reply that explains the decision of the library concerning the resource in question. The American Library Association Office for Intellectual Freedom is an important resource for all libraries. When there are difficult decisions to be made, they should be consulted since they bring to the issue a great deal of experience.

Outline of a Collection Development Policy/Statement

Collection development policies/statements cover much of what is in this chapter. It usually has the following parts:

1. Purpose of the policy/statement. This is usually an overview statement that tells everyone why there is a policy/statement and how the policy/statement will be used.

2. Library mission, goals, and objectives. The reason for stating the library's mission, goals, and objectives is to provide context for how the library views itself and its relationship to the collection.

3. Overview of the collection. This will provide information about the collection in general. It will discuss what subjects are emphasized in the collection and which are less important. It will include information about the collection's strengths and weaknesses. It is important to mention what subject areas are not collected and why. It could be because of a nearby collection in that area or simply because it's not a subject of great interest to the community. Perhaps the library does not purchase law books because there is a law library nearby or does not collect local

history materials because there is a library at the local historical society.

4. Who is responsible for collection development. Often the director is responsible for the collection, but usually the director has delegated to a staff member the responsibility for the collection.

5. The organization of selection. Libraries have many ways to organize selection, so it is important to say how selection is organized in a particular library. It might be centralized selection or it might be title-by-title selection in branches or departments.

6. Information about the community served. This can be a general description of the community—its interests and census information. It will offer some clues as to what the library's priorities are. For example, if there is a large population of children and teens, the library will spend more of its budget in that area.

7. Information on the budget and funding sources. Most people do not know much about the library's funding, so here is one place to discuss how the collection is funded. It is often a combination of local government funding and maybe some additional funding from the state as well as some bequests, gifts, and grants.

8. Selection criteria. Selection criteria are an important part of the policy/statement. Patrons and staff members alike need to know how the library selects materials and what the most important criteria are. Listing the criteria is very important. The criteria might include writing style, accuracy, currency, appropriate for intended age level, and coverage of subject.

9. What formats the library collects and why. It is important to list the formats included in the collection. Formats are constantly changing so the policy/statement must also change. This section can explain that some formats are no longer available and have been replaced by another format. For example, the library no longer acquires cassettes and instead collects CDs.

10. Cooperative arrangements. If the library has cooperative arrangements with other libraries, they should be listed in the policy/statement. This could be the case with electronic data-

bases and other e-reference books, which are available through a library group or consortium. It is a good piece of information for everyone to have.

11. Intellectual freedom issues. For a public library it is important to state that they support the ALA Bill of Rights and the ALA Freedom to Read statement. Public libraries strive to collect materials for all interests, so it is only logical that some materials will offend some patrons. The library will want to provide a way for patrons to challenge materials in the library. The library should be prepared with a form that the user can fill out, stating their objection to a particular item and a stated process that the library will follow in evaluating the complaint and reporting to the user.

12. How the library handles gifts. Libraries receive many gifts. Some are just used books that the library may not want to add to the collection, while others are more valuable materials. It is important to inform patrons how the library will deal with gift books. There may be one way to handle used books and another for more valuable materials. It is important that the library state that once materials are given to the library, they are owned by the library and the library can make decisions as to how to use or dispose of them.

13. Collection maintenance—weeding and storage issues. Weeding is one of most sensitive issues in the library, so it is important to state what the criteria are for discarding materials. These criteria might include out of date, poor condition, and inaccurate information. Sometimes libraries choose to store materials. Once again, it is a good idea to state why some books or other materials are stored and how the user can retrieve them for their use.

14. Collection evaluation. Libraries must evaluate their collections from time to time to see if materials need to be withdrawn, replaced, or stored. It is important to explain this process so that patrons are aware of the library's procedures.

A sample collection development policy is provided at the end of this chapter.

In summary, collection development and collection management are of prime importance to public libraries. Even though there are now many other programs and services in public libraries, patrons expect to find an up-to-date collection of books and other materials such as audio and video materials and e-collections. Most public libraries continue to have a less-than-adequate materials budget, so selection of materials must be made carefully, which is often title by title. Public libraries are adding materials to their collections to meet requests for current information, they are not building research collections. In contrast to academic libraries that build collections for the future, public libraries are oriented to the present, and consequently they also discard materials that are dated or now hold no interest for their patrons.

Discussion Questions

1. How would you decide how to balance the purchase of physical items for the library's collection versus subscribing to e-materials?

2. How would you handle a complaint about material that the library owns?

Beaverton City Library Gift Policy

Adopted by the Beaverton City Library Advisory Board November 2016

The Beaverton City Library welcomes gifts of library materials, money, or real property that will enrich library resources and help the library better serve the needs of the community. Donations are considered outright and unrestricted. The library reserves the right to accept or decline a gift, donation, endowment, bequest, or trust. When funds are donated for a specific purpose, the amount and nature of the expenditure must be approved in advance by the city. As a department of city government, donations are tax deductible to the fullest extent provided by law. A receipt for tax purposes will be provided upon request; library staff cannot appraise the value of donations.

Monetary and Real Property Gifts

Monetary gifts will be utilized by the library to purchase materials or equipment, support library programs, or in other ways the Library Advisory Board and the city deem appropriate. The library welcomes gifts of cash for the direct purchase of library materials and will try to accommodate the subject or title preferences of the donor in so far as they meet standards established in the Collection Development Policy. Donations of substantial cash offerings, securities, real property, art, and bequests will be handled by the library director, who, with the Library Advisory Board, will work out terms of acceptance compatible with library policies, the donor's intent, city policy, and applicable laws.

Books and Other Library Materials

The library welcomes gifts of print and nonprint materials with the understanding that gifts of materials will be added to the collection only if they meet the same criteria for inclusion in and withdrawal from the collection as purchased materials. Donated materials are considered the sole property of the library, and the library does not accept responsibility for notifying donors of the disposition of donated materials. Gift materials not added to the collection may be given to the New Friends of the Beaverton City Library for resale, donated to other libraries or organizations, recycled, or discarded.

Madison (Wisconsin) Public Library Collection Development Policy

I. The Policy

The Madison Public Library Collection Development Policy provides a framework for the growth and development of collections in support of the Library's mission to "provide free and equitable access to cultural and educational experiences and celebrate ideas, promote creativity, connect people, and enrich lives."

It is the Library's goal to provide a diverse Madison community with library materials that reflect a wide range of views, expressions, opinions and interests. Specific acquisitions may include items that may be unorthodox or unpopular with the majority or controversial in nature. The Library's acquisition of these items does not constitute endorsement of their content but rather makes available its expression.

The Library provides free access to materials in a number of formats (print, media and electronic) to all customers. Library users make their own choices as to what they will use based on individual interests and concerns. Madison Public Library supports the right of each family to decide which items are appropriate for use by their children. Responsibility for a child's use of library materials lies with his or her parent or guardian. Madison Public Library adheres to the principles of intellectual freedom, adopted by the American Library Association, as expressed in the Library Bill of Rights and the Freedom to Read and Freedom to View Statements.

II. About the Library and Its Community

Madison is a city with a unique culture. It's home to a world-class university, a growing bio-tech industry, the seat of state government, and a growing and increasingly diverse population—culturally, linguistically and ethnically. Madison is a highly educated community and people in Madison make good use of their public libraries. Still, challenges remain. Families in poverty are a concern—43% of children in the public schools qualify for free lunch. The number of people whose first language is not English and the issues of early literacy and school readiness require targeted public library collections and services.

The Madison Public Library consists of a Central Library and eight neighborhood libraries. As well as serving the needs and interests of people who live and work downtown, the Central Library provides extensive, in-depth collections and centralized support for library services throughout the City. The Central Library is also the resource library for all public libraries in the seven-county South Central Library System, all of which have access to the more than 500,000 general, specialized and historic items in its collection. The neighborhood libraries provide collections and a full range of services to the people in their immediately adjacent neighborhoods; they also attract substantial use from a larger geographical area, to a greater or lesser degree, depending on their unique circumstances of site, convenience and access.

III. The Collection

Madison Public Library's collection of approximately one million books and other media provides a wide range of literary, cultural, educational, informational and recreational materials for people of all ages. Collections include popular and in-demand materials as well as special formats, such as large print books, government documents, foreign language materials, test and study guides, financial, tax and business information, company and telephone directories, school and career information, consumer, health and medical information. In addition, the Local Materials Collection preserves and documents the history of Madison and Dane County and provides a broad scope of information about local news, events and businesses.

The variety of formats collected include:

- Print: books, documents, magazines, newspapers, pamphlets, and maps.

- Audiovisual Media: videos on DVD and Blu-ray, books on CD and digital audio player, music on compact disc.

- Electronic Media: databases, software, electronic books, downloadable audio books, videos and music. The library also provides access to the internet. Selected internet sites are cataloged and linked to the Library's website.

- Other: multimedia kits, microforms, educational toys, devices for the visually impaired, and selected audiovisual equipment.

IV. Criteria for Selection

General criteria for selecting library materials are listed below. An item need not meet all of the criteria in order to be acceptable.

- public demand, interest or need

- contemporary significance, popular interest or permanent value

- attention of critics and reviewers

- prominence, authority and/or competence of author, creator or publisher

- timeliness of material

- relation to existing collections

- statement of challenging, original, or alternative point of view

- authenticity of historical, regional or social setting

- accessibility for multiple users of electronic formats

V. MPL Website

The Madison Public Library website provides a link to LINKcat, the on-line catalog of materials and to other electronic resources. It also offers links to subject-focused websites recommended by professional staff. In linking other websites to its home pages the Library follows the selection criteria cited above. Beyond this, the Library has not participated in the development of these other sites and does not exert any editorial or other control over these sites. Any link from the Library's website to another website is not an endorsement from the Library. The Library does not warrant that its website, the server that makes it available, or any links from its site to other websites are free of viruses or other harmful components.

VI. Responsibility for Selection

Responsibility for the initial selection of library resources rests with the Library's professional staff, based on the criteria cited above. Designated staff are responsible for specific areas of the collection, under the overall direction of the Library Collection Manager. The responsibility for selection ultimately rests with the Library Director operating within the framework of policies determined by the Board of the Madison Public Library.

VII. Suggestions for Additions to the Collection

To assure the acquisition of resources desired by Library users, customer suggestions are always considered for their addition to the collection. Customers can request that specific items be purchased by filling out a Recommendation for Purchase form online or at any Madison Public Library location.

VIII. Collection Maintenance, Replacement and Weeding

Professional library staff regularly review items in the collection to ensure that they continue to meet customers' needs. Materials that are worn, obsolete, unused, old editions or unnecessarily duplicated are removed. It is the responsibility of professional staff to assess the need for replacing materials that are damaged, destroyed or lost. Items are not automatically replaced. Decisions are based on need, demand and budget.

IX. Gifts

Madison Public Library accepts gifts of new or gently-used books, magazines, DVDs, and music or books on compact disc. Decisions on whether and how donated items will be added to the Library's collections are based on the same evaluative criteria that are applied to purchased materials.

With rare exceptions, we do not return items that are given to us. Items that are not added to the collections are given to the Friends groups supporting Madison Public Library.

X. Request for Reconsideration of Materials

The Library welcomes citizens' expressions of opinion concerning materials purchased. Requests to remove materials will be considered within the context of the policies set forth in this document. Anyone who wishes to request that a specific item be reconsidered for inclusion in the collection of materials is asked to complete and sign the Request for Reconsideration Form, available at any Madison Public Library location. The form will be forwarded to the Library Collection Manager for adult materials and children's materials, who will consider the request in a timely fashion, in consultation with the director. The questioned material will be reviewed, in its entirety, and once a decision has been made regarding the retention or removal of the material, a letter will be sent to the person, explaining the decision. If the person indicates dissatisfaction with the resolution, he/she may appeal to the Library Board. The Board will reconsider the decision based on whether or not the particular title conforms to the Board-approved Collection Development Policy, as outlined in the "Criteria for Selection," above.

This policy was approved by the Library Board on December 1, 2016

Bibliography

American Library Association. n.d. "Office for Intellectual Freedom." Accessed December 14, 2020. http://www.ala.org/aboutala/offices/oif.

Bradford, Robin. 2019. "Modern Collection Development: The Mission Remains the Same." *Public Libraries* 58 (1): 33–36.

Johnson, Peggy. 2014. *Fundamentals of Collection Development and Management*, 3rd ed. Chicago: American Library Association.

Larson, Jeanette. 2012. *CREW: A Weeding Manual for Modern Libraries*. Austin: Texas State Library and Archives Commission.

MARKETING AND PROMOTION

- Our competition
- Marketing theory
- Marketing plans
- Brand identity
- Market segmentation
- The four Ps: product, place, price, and promotion
- Case studies

Today, competition for attention is a way of life. Every day, institutions and organizations develop new and unique ways of promoting themselves. In order to continue to get attention from the public, an institution must continually call attention to itself in a variety of ways. For example, Honda recently ran an ad using Italian opera singers just to get people's attention. It is not enough to provide good resources and solid services. The institution, and in this case the library, has to develop a way to bring its resources and services to the attention of its users on a regular basis. The library and its products must be out in front of the public, reminding people they are still in business and that they have products that will be useful to many people.

Our Competition

Public libraries once thought they were so unique that they did not have to market their materials and services because no one else provided free materials and information services. But that was before Google. Google provides an easy way to get an answer quickly. Maybe it is not the most thorough answer, nor even a completely accurate answer. But it provides a "good enough" answer. So ever since Google began, libraries have tried often unsuccessfully to explain how they differed from Google. People still need books, articles, and information. But now there are Google Books and Google Scholar. Although everything is not free or even easily available, still many try Google before going any place else. After all, one can do a Google search at home or in the office. Librarians all know there is more to finding information than just Google, so how can this be explained to the public? Many of the answers will be in this chapter, so do read on.

Libraries provide many unique materials and services to their community. Once potential users are introduced to the library, they are often thrilled and wonder why they didn't know about them. Yet sometimes using the library is just more difficult than using Google and more time consuming, and that extra ounce of energy needed may mean that the user chooses not to use the library. So how can the library overcome this and thus gain and keep a new audience? Personalized services in the library, such as sitting down with a librarian to discuss how to approach a particular project or by phone or by web-based services, will often provide just what the user needs. Libraries have always been more than a warehouse of resources, but they have not necessarily made it clear to their users.

Marketing Theory

Today, writers on marketing such as Philip Kotler state that "the role of marketers is to guide customers throughout their journey from awareness to advocacy" (Kotler, Kartajaya, and Setiawan 2017, xvi). This is because there are an increasing number of sites where people can chat, including Facebook and Twitter, and customers now pay more attention to the opinions of others, especially family and friends, than they do to traditional marketing. This does not mean there is no role for traditional marketing. But it does mean it is important to look at the various channels for marketing, including television, radio, print sources, internet, and social media. A combination of marketing channels must be used in order to reach the many possible customers. People are gathering information about products and services from many places and from many people, but especially from their relatives, friends, and neighbors. Marketers now understand that "the best source of influence is the army of customers turned advocates" (Kotler, Kartajaya, and Setiawan 2017, 59). It is, therefore, important that libraries develop advocates who can carry the message about libraries to others. This happens by having satisfied customers and through library users, a Friends group, and library partners.

Content marketing can also play a role in this world where a mix of the traditional marketing and digital marketing coexist. People want more than a clever slogan. They want more detailed information about what is being offered to them. Often customers telling stories about what they found useful at the library or simply the opinion of others as to what the library offers to its customers can be very meaningful to a customer trying to make a decision. Good library stories can be posted on the library's website or on a social media channel such as Facebook.

> Library stories can be an opportunity to teach the value of libraries to . . . (community) leaders. . . . We need to touch the hearts of our funders with the well-constructed narrative of the child reading to a dog; the displaced worker who comes to the library learns how to complete a resume, fill out a job application online, and returns to share that they found a job; the mom who learned how to play with her child and prepares that child for a life of learning; or that same mom socializing with other moms after story time. (Eicher-Catt and Edmonson 2016, 219)

Stories present a more human touch that relates more closely to a person's life and experience. Gathering stories is an important way to reach out to present and prospective users.

Marketing Plans

Planning is the key to successful marketing. Certainly all libraries have a few good marketing ideas they can try. Library marketing cannot be haphazard but rather must be planned. Spontaneity is fine, but it does not replace a marketing plan. The plan should be both long and short range. Here are some reasons libraries should develop a marketing strategy or plan.

Libraries need to reach their users on a regular basis, reminding them of the services and resources they provide. People lead busy lives and can easily forget how helpful the library can be in solving daily problems. The reminders about library resources and services can come in many forms: an online newsletter, a text, a blog, a notice on social media (Facebook, Instagram, etc.), or information on the library's website. If one looks at other nonprofit organizations, they change their message from time to time. Libraries must do the same. There are many ways to talk about library resources and services so the message is varied throughout the year, keeping the public interested in what the library has to offer. Now that books, articles, and information are widely available, what makes the library different are the expensive databases and other services it provides to the user. Public libraries must articulate their services, such as being able to get the text of an article the user wants, read an e-book, borrow a book not available locally, listen to streaming music, find the best resources on a particular subject, and attend an online program, such as a book discussion group or a presentation by an author.

Libraries must find out what their users need and provide their users with resources and services that meet their present and future needs. In libraries there has been a shift from "just in case" collections to "just in time" collections. It is great to collect with the "long tail" idea; that is, people may want that less-than-popular book that the library bought "in case" someone wanted it. But more and more it may become uneconomical to do this on a large scale. Libraries will want to listen more closely to what their users are saying about their information needs and try to meet those needs, even if they are not the image of what the library does. Libraries will have to conduct surveys more often, run focus groups, and even do interviews with stakeholders in order to understand where the library fits in.

Here are some guidelines for developing a marketing plan:

- Define the library's marketing goals.

- Define the library's marketing objectives.

- Use surveys, focus groups, interviews, and so forth to find out more about user needs and interests.

- Identify local influencers whom your users respect.

- Define the library's target audience(s).

- Define possible niche audience(s).

- Select the best ways to deliver content to the library's audience(s). This is now a mix of the traditional channels of communication, digital resources, and social media.

Libraries need to maintain a high positive profile, keeping people aware of their programs and services. This can help them combat attempts to reduce their budgets. Libraries have suffered many budget cuts in the last few years. Although some have successfully fought off the cuts, perhaps they would not have been so vulnerable to cuts if they had had a higher profile. Sometimes public libraries go about their work so quietly that the public does not understand what services libraries offer and that many services can be quickly provided. Libraries need to promote themselves more effectively and to be as transparent as possible. All promotion need not be expensive. With all the social networking tools available, libraries can reach out to their many audiences through Facebook, Twitter, blogs, and more.

Libraries have to tell their story over and over again using both factual information and anecdotal information. Think about the number of ads on television that tell the story of one or two users of the services that the institution is promoting. Personal stories are so effective. Libraries have many personal stories about how the library has helped users solve their problems. It can be the person who found a job because the library helped him redo his résumé or the immigrant grandmother who can read to her grandchild because there are bilingual children's books. Visual marketing is an important component, so try to get a user to tell their own story.

Some of the ways the library can communicate with their patrons are as follows:

- eNewletters: one for the library as a whole or maybe separate ones for some parts of the public, such as children or the business community

- Press releases

- Public service announcements

- Website

- Radio

- Television

- Social media, including Facebook, Twitter, YouTube, Instagram

- Posters and fliers

- In-house signage

- Advertising in newspapers and magazines

- Emails to patrons

- Direct mail to patrons

- Presentations to local groups

Brand Identity

Libraries need to develop a brand identity. Strong brands have an identity that can be recognized immediately, and libraries need this too. The American Library Association developed the "@ the library" campaign, which was a way that libraries could adopt a brand with a nationwide identity. In a local branding effort the County of Los Angeles Library changed its name to the Los Angeles County Library and added this very creative slogan: "Curiosity Welcome."

Whether it is the ALA brand or a local branding, libraries need something identifiable so that when they provide information about their resources and services, their users will immediately know it is a message from the library. Consistency in branding is very important. It cannot be overemphasized that each piece from the library, whether written or audio or video, must include the branding. The branding can be a logo or a slogan or both.

Here are examples of library branding:

Figure 11.1. Libraries present themselves through their logos. Here are examples: the Miami-Dade Public Library System and Princeton Public Library. *Courtesy of Miami-Dade Public Library System, Florida; Princeton Public Library, New Jersey.*

Market Segmentation

Libraries can do a lot or a little market segmentation. It is obvious that public libraries have a wide range of audiences to reach who are not all interested in the same thing. Children, teens, and adults all have different needs. Even within the area of services to children there are very young children, preschool children, and school-age children who all have different interests and different reading levels. Adults come with a wide range of interests both in terms of reading material and in terms of programming. Adults may have interests related to their work or to their leisure time. Younger adults will have different interests from senior citizens, although it is possible that on some issues they will all be interested in the same subject areas. It is good to collect lists of patrons who can be grouped together so that the library can send out targeted messages, especially for programming.

The Four Ps: Product, Place, Price, and Promotion

Marketing always talks about the four Ps: product, place, price, and promotion. It is important to look at each of them in relation to libraries.

Libraries have many more products to offer than they ever had before. Beyond books (print and e-books) there are audio products (audiobooks, streaming audio, and music); video products (DVDs, streaming video); digital products (databases, etc.); many useful items such as are in the Library of Things, which might include items for cooking that are only used on occasion, bicycle repair kits, air quality monitors, or gardening items; and programs.

Place is also a larger concept that in previous times. Place can be the physical building(s), but it can also be the many offerings provided digitally and online so that the user does not have to leave home or library programs presented at other community locations.

For library users the price is usually free. But sometimes a special program or some special service may come at a reasonable price.

Libraries need to promote their services to different user audiences. All marketing plans develop promotion for different audiences. Libraries have often not targeted their services to different groups. Yet, not everyone using the library wants the same resources and services; despite this, libraries have used one message for all. Older adults use different services than do parents, teachers use different services than do students, older adults want different services than do younger adults, and researchers want different services than do business people. So a more varied message can reach a diverse audience more effectively. Some libraries have tried to package their services to reach parts of their user group and have developed a number of websites. For example, the Denver Public Library has a number of websites, some of which are aimed at particular groups, such as children, teens, or people who speak Spanish, or to highlight special collections, such as digital collections. All libraries need to find ways to reach out to their many audiences. The more segmented the library's marketing, the more it can appeal to certain user groups.

Libraries need to evaluate their competition and plan their promotion accordingly. Libraries do have a unique product. Yet in our fast-paced world people may think library services are too slow and cumbersome. But this is not always the case. People who have not used libraries recently will be pleasantly surprised at the changes in library services. Librarians need to think about how their services can change to meet the demands of their users for quicker and more convenient services.

Case Studies

An article by Citlin Cowart (2017) discusses the marketing strategies used at the San Antonio Public Library where they have a team of nonlibrarian marketing specialists. Their initial effort was to develop the Digital Library Community Project. To increase public awareness of the library's digital resources, they developed a series of "Digital Library wallpapers." Each of the wallpapers was designed to look like library bookshelves and was placed in one of the library's community partner's buildings. Also, three digital touch screen kiosks were placed at the San Antonio Airport where people could borrow e-books and e-audiobooks. In addition to developing public awareness of the digital collection, the library wanted to increase use of the digital collection, and they have been successful at doing this. The third goal was to identify new audiences. The library developed pages on Facebook, Instagram, Pinterest, Snapchat, Twitter, and YouTube. This helped them to reach the millennials. They found that their largest audience was women from twenty-five to forty-five with children. Through social media the library could present curated e-reading lists for adults and children and also provide users the opportunity to communicate one to one with a librarian. Finally, the library developed a mobile app to encourage the use of the library. The users through the app could browse, place holds, and access account information. As this project has matured, the library has worked with many local organizations developing curated collections for special events, reaching out to organizations who have members with similar interests, working more with the media, and training others such as the Library Friends group to market to their networks.

The Austin Public Library developed an ambassador program to expand its coverage of social media. Library users can sign up to be an ambassador for the library. They provide their name, their email, and information about where they can help the library on social media. They are asked to add the library to their social media platforms. Then the library sends them information about programs and projects that they are asked to post on the social media they use. They are also encouraged to share stories about the library on social media. From time to time the ambassadors are invited to something special at the library, such as a preview of the renovated Central Library before it opened. This ambassador's group acts as a circle of trust for the library and provides an awareness of what is happening at the library. Other libraries have followed this example (Garza 2019).

In conclusion, public libraries are making good strides to make themselves more visible in the community. They now provide more information on their websites as to how to access e-books and even how to connect to online programs. Local residents are realizing that libraries provide a wide variety of resources, programs, and services free of charge and available as close as their computer. Libraries offer a wide assortment of resources for all ages. Continuing their strong marketing will assist libraries in being well regarded in their communities and strengthen their ability to get needed funding. But good marketing means continually changing and adding to the message.

Discussion Questions

1. What are effective ways to reach the library's audiences?

2. How could the library further expand its marketing?

Bibliography

Cowart, Citlin. 2017. "Marketing Is a Team Effort." *RUSA* 56 (4): 240–44.
Eicher-Catt, Deborah, and Mina Edmonson. 2016. "Reimagining Public Libraries as Learning Communities: What Library Stories Can Tell Us." *Public Library Quarterly* 35 (3): 205–21.

Garza, Cesar. 2019. "Why Your Library Needs Social Media Ambassadors Now." *Texas Library Journal* 95, no. 4 (Winter): 8–10.

Kotler, Philip. 2011. "Reinventing Marketing to Manage the Environmental Imperative." *Journal of Marketing* 75, no. 4 (July): 132–36.

Kotler, Philip, Hermawan Kartajaya, and Iwan Setiawan. 2017. *Marketing 4.0: Moving from Traditional to Digital*. New York: Wiley.

Perreault, William D., Jr., Joseph P. Cannon, and E. Jerome McCarthy. 2008. *Basic Marketing: A Marketing Strategy Planning Approach*, 16th ed. New York: McGraw-Hill/Irwin.

THE POSTPANDEMIC PUBLIC LIBRARY

- Collections
- Programs and services
- Space
- Human-centered design
- Coping with change
- Sustainability
- Access to online resources
- Looking at trends

This book has examined many aspects of public libraries from their history to their governance, finances, and development of collections, services, and programs for all ages. Libraries changed in many ways in the twentieth century, and now in the twenty-first century more changes are in store. In the early part of the twentieth century, many more public libraries were built starting with funding from Andrew Carnegie. People wanted to read and enjoyed having access to public libraries that offered them a wide variety of reading materials at no cost. Public libraries are often the only institution in a community that is open to all at no cost. In addition to access to their buildings, public libraries serve users with bookmobiles, deposit collections, outreach to community centers, and even home deliveries. During the second half of the twentieth century, public libraries adopted new technology including automated circulation systems, online public access catalogs, and new ways of providing information through online databases and e-books. New structures for public library funding were developed at the state and national levels to supplement local funding. By the end of the twentieth century, most libraries provided computers and access to the internet for their users.

Libraries have supported intellectual freedom as its principles are stated in the Freedom to Read statement and the Library Bill of Rights and have held to their principles to provide a wide variety of reading material from different points of view. This has not always been easy, and with the advent of access to the internet, libraries faced many difficult questions since the subjects the users chose to explore went beyond the subjects available at the library. But intellectual freedom has continued to be an important principle for all libraries.

Seeing into the future is not easy as the United States continues to battle the COVID-19 pandemic. It is obvious that public libraries are changing in both the short and the long run. More information will be online than ever before—not just collections but programs and services as well. Much will depend on the public and how they envision their public libraries and how they want to use them in the future. The public has proven themselves flexible and resilient during the pandemic, and they will no doubt be flexible about the public library's future plans and offerings. But what we do know is that "the balance between physical materials, virtual materials, learning opportunities, events and social interactions is in flux" (McCarthy 2018, 248).

Collections

U.S. publishing has continued to increase so that more publications are available for libraries to acquire to meet the very diverse interests of the American people. In 1910, about 13,500 books were published each year (Martin 1998), and by the end of the century, more than 200,000 books were being published annually. This great expansion in publishing has given public libraries the opportunity to enrich their print collections and to add audiovisual material and e-books. Public libraries in the last quarter of the twentieth century began to add more books in other languages as new immigrants wanted to continue to read in their native languages. Books were also added in large print for those with vision problems. The publishing of children's books had been encouraged by the development of children's services in the first quarter of the twentieth century, but young adult book publishing came later and is now a vibrant part of the publishing scene. Many authors have begun to self-publish while others remain with large and small publishing companies.

Public library collections are robust, with most libraries purchasing multiple copies of the most popular titles. Books are now available in several formats, making it possible for users to have their choice of

- print,
- e-books,
- audiobooks,
- video, and
- large print books.

This trend will continue for the immediate future. Although e-books are becoming more popular, other formats continue to be requested by users.

Programs and Services

Public library programming is now a major part of library service. Programming highlights the many subjects in collections in libraries for

- education,
- recreation, and
- information.

Programming presents an opportunity for users to discuss current issues, learn about impending issues, hear authors read and discuss their books, see old and new films, and learn new skills, such as new computer programs available at training sessions. Makerspaces in public libraries have provided users with the opportunity to try new technology such as 3D printers and learn new skills such as coding. Programs such as makerspaces can supplement and expand the information in books and give users a chance to explore new ideas on their own or to work collaboratively with others. Libraries began to provide a wide range of online programs during the pandemic. The future may mean that libraries will continue to hold some programs online and other programs will be face-to-face.

Public libraries are providing groups with a space to meet. It could be a group of mothers doing homeschooling for their children or a community group that has no place for their monthly meetings. Some libraries have built a special room that individuals or groups can use to make recordings or videos. Communities are always in need of space, and libraries can be a source.

Brian Kenney (2020), director of the White Plains (New York) Public Library, reported the following: "The formula is simple: the community still wants to come together, learn, and share with one another through the library. Programs like Zoom make it easier than ever to support scores of discussion groups. And the flexibility of online programming—and the record-setting attendance—means there's likely no going back for many library events."

Space

Space is a precious commodity in libraries. Space consultants suggest that libraries should downsize their collections to open up more space, especially since parts of public library collections seldom circulate. New renovations have also opted for furniture on wheels so that the floors of the library can be more flexible. Shelving, service points such as reference desks, computer workstations, and other furniture are all now available on wheels, allowing more flexibility for the library. This makes it possible to reconfigure a floor of the library and allow for more creative uses.

Human-Centered Design

Beginning with the Aarhus Library in Denmark and its collaboration with the Chicago Public Library, libraries have begun to talk about human-centered design. In human-centered design, libraries listen to their users, observe their users, ask strategic questions, and think through possible changes that will benefit their users. Human-centered design goes beyond just adding more technology to making changes that address problems brought to the attention of the library by the public. Libraries need to better understand how different generations use public libraries and try to accommodate the different ways they are being used.

Coping with Change

Public libraries have shown themselves to be swift and flexible as new challenges have arisen. They have adapted to new technology, answered questions online and through social media, and publicized their libraries on social media such as Facebook and Twitter, added materials in new formats, and now libraries are adapting to protect the health of their staff and users. The COVID-19 pandemic caused public libraries to close, but many found new ways to serve their users. Users requested titles, and libraries allowed them to pick up their requests outside the library. Users missed the library's programs so the programs went online. There were story hours for children both online and by phone, book discussions for adults, and even speakers that users could view online. Some libraries now have their own channel on YouTube. Libraries even experimented with delivering books by drone and providing summer educational programs for children online.

Sustainability

In the middle of the many issues facing libraries, sustainability is of continuing importance. Climate change is a big consideration in building and renovating libraries. Libraries must think about the best way to conserve energy in heating, lighting, and use of space. Flexibility in space use will be important for the future. "Open library space . . . (can) promote creativity, innovation and participatory interaction among library constituents" (Eicher-Catt and Edmonson 2016, 217). There is much for libraries to consider.

Access to Online Resources

Although access to online resources was always considered of utmost importance, the pandemic and the need to find materials online, the need for school-age children to be able to access their classes from home, and the need for many to be able to use telemedicine brought a new reality. Public library directors soon realized that not everyone had internet access. So in association with other community partners many libraries have worked to make access possible in every part of the region they serve. Both internet access and digital literacy remain a priority to be achieved. In some communities libraries have tried to provide temporary access through internet access on vans, extending the library's Wi-Fi further, providing hot spots, and so forth.

Looking at Trends

The future is hard to predict. We can look out a few years, but we know that change is always there and there can suddenly be another pandemic or a weather event that is going to change everything. Planning is important; although things may change, libraries still need to plan ahead. Trends can be looked at from three points of view:

- people,

- technology, and

- collections and services.

Much has changed in people's lives. Many are living on their own, while others have formed untraditional groups to live together. More people have started their own businesses working from their homes, while others work for companies that allow them to work from home most of the time or full time. People make the best of their leisure time by traveling or by spending time in a more relaxed place.

Technology is always changing. People use mobile devices constantly and want to be able to use them to reach the library to put a hold on a book, to get a question answered by a librarian, or to check the online catalog. Users don't need to borrow audiovisual materials when they can get them virtually and listen or view them streaming. Users are willing to put e-books on their mobile phones and read them there. They also like all the things they can explore with the makerspaces.

Communities have changed too. There is a lot more diversity of interests. Some people are moving ahead and prefer using the library virtually, while others prefer the more traditional library. Both options need to be available to meet the diverse needs and interests of the community.

Bibliography

Eicher-Catt, Deborah, and Mina Edmonson. 2016. "Reimagining Public Libraries as Learning Communities: What Library Stories Can Tell Us." *Public Library Quarterly* 35 (3): 205–21.

Kenney, Brian. 2020. "The Library Is Open (Sort Of . . .)." *Publishers Weekly*, August 21. https://www.publishersweekly.com/pw/by-topic/industry-news/libraries/article/84151-the-library-is-open-sort-of.html.

Martin, Lowell A. 1998. *Enrichment: A History of the Public Library in the United States in the Twentieth Century.* Metuchen, NJ: Scarecrow Press.

McCarthy, Richard. 2018. "Future Proofing Your Public Library." *Public Library Quarterly* 37 (3): 248–62.

INDEX

Page references for figures are italicized.

ABOUT THE AUTHOR

Kay Ann Cassell is an adjunct professor at the Rutgers University Department of Library and Information Science where she teaches a variety of courses, including reference and information services, collection development, and public libraries. She has worked in public and academic libraries. She has been the director of the Bethlehem (New York) Public Library, the director of the Huntington (New York) Public Library, the director of the New School for Social Research library, and the associate director for collections and services at the New York Public Library (NYPL). As NYPL's associate director of collections and services, she oversaw the development of reference services, collections, programs, and services for all branches. She has also worked as a coordinator for public library services at the New Jersey State Library and the Westchester Library System. Cassell is the coauthor of *Reference and Information Services: An Introduction* and the author of *Managing Reference Today*.